Hillary's Pursuit of Power

Hillary's Pursuit of Power

Jerry Zeifman

Copyright © 2006 by Jerry Zeifman.

ISBN 10:   Softcover   1-4257-1791-8

ISBN 13:   Softcover   978-1-4257-1791-9

All rights reserved. No part of this publication may be reproduced or transmitted in any form or by any means electronic or mechanical, including photocopy, recording, or any information storage and retrieval system now known or be invented, without permission in writing from the author, except by a reviewer who wishes to quote brief passages in connection with a review written for inclusion in a magazine, newspaper, or broadcast.

This book was printed in the United States of America.

To order additional copies of this book, contact:
Xlibris Corporation
1-888-795-4274
www.Xlibris.com
Orders@Xlibris.com
34338

Contents

Preface 11
Prologue 13

PART ONE
The Nixon Impeachment

1   The New Chairman 17
2   Cancer on the Presidency 19
3   Secret Tapes, Deep Throat, and the CIA 21
4   The Ford Confirmation and the Firing of Cox 23
5   Impeachment Begins 29
6   John Doar 32
7   Hillary and Her Role Models 35
8   The Strategy of Delay 38
9   Thrusting Greatness on Rodino 41
10 The "Smoking Gun" 45
11 Hillary's Secret Book 47

PART TWO
The Clinton Presidency

12 Ascent to Power 53
13 Hillary and Health Care 56
14 Friends in Office 58
15 Whitewater 62
16 Webster Hubbell 66
17 An Indonesian Monopoly 68
18 The China Connection 70
19 Other Foreign Policies 74

20	"Citizenship USA"	77
21	White House for Sale	79
22	Leaving the White House	83

Notes 87
Bibliography 91

In memory of my mentor,
House Judiciary Committee chairman
Emanuel Celler (D—NY),
who served in Congress for 50 years,
and whose autobiography is entitled,
You Never Leave Brooklyn

**Acclaim for Jerry Zeifman's prior book *Without Honor:
The Crimes of Camelot and the Impeachment of President Nixon***

This behind-the-scenes look at the infamous Watergate scandals provides compelling first-hand knowledge that both Democrats loyal to the Kennedys and Republicans "stonewalled" the investigation of President Nixon . . . There are also cameo appearances by Hillary Clinton. Her actions reveal that if she is not a liar, at least she has no interest in justice . . . Highly recommended.
Five Star Review
Amazon.com

I got a kick out of *Without Honor*. I liked it a lot. I sometimes try to imagine myself functioning in the political circles of Washington. I wouldn't have had the patience to cope with it. They would have had to send me home in a wheel chair.
Saul Bellow (Nobel Laureate)

A cogent blockbuster
Publishers Weekly

The story is utterly fascinating and the extraordinary quotes from his diary taped at the time surely make it a primary source of considerable importance.
Edward Mortimer
Financial Times of London

After I started Jerry Zeifman's extraordinarily insightful book I could not put it down—and finished it in one sitting.
Henry Hyde
Chairman, House Judiciary Committee

Preface

At the time of Watergate I had supervisory authority over the House Judiciary Committee's Impeachment Inquiry staff—on which Hillary Clinton and Bernard Nussbaum served. I then kept a private diary which is now in the Watergate Collection of the George Washington University Library. Excerpts from my diary comprise a portion of this book.

After President Nixon's resignation a young lawyer who shared an office with Hillary, confided in me that he was dismayed by her erroneous legal opinions and efforts to deny Nixon representation by counsel, as well as by Nussbaum's unwillingness to investigate Nixon. In my diary I noted the following:

August 12, 1974—John Labovitz apologized to me for the fact that months ago he and Hillary had lied to me [to conceal rules changes and dilatory tactics.] *Labovitz said. "That came from Yale." I said "You mean Burke Marshall* [Senator Ted Kennedy's chief political strategist, with whom Hillary regularly consulted in violation of House rules.] *Labovitz said, "Yes." His apology was significant to me, not because it was a revelation but because of his contrition.*

Because of a number of her unethical practices I eventually decided that I could not recommend Hillary for any subsequent position of public or private trust. I also took the same position regarding her immediate supervisor, Bernie Nussbaum.

Two decades later Bill Clinton became President. He gave Hillary an office in the West Wing of the White House, with considerable authority over his staff. He also appointed Bernie Nussbaum as his chief White House counsel, with an office next to Hillary's. Some months later Nussbaum was forced to resign after a New York Times editorial charged him with ethical violations. Hillary also became controversial. William Safire of the New York Times called her "a congenital liar."

Throughout the entire eight years of the Clinton presidency Hillary's conduct confirmed my earlier assessment of the ethical flaws in her character.

Prologue

In 1973 Senator Ted Kennedy, Yale Professor Burke Marshall, and other Kennedy supporters persuaded House Judiciary Committee chairman, Peter Rodino, to appoint John Doar to head our Nixon Impeachment Inquiry Staff. Ten years earlier Marshall had been Assistant Attorney General in the Kennedy Department of Justice and Doar had been his deputy.

At Yale Marshall's students had nicknamed him "The Attorney General in waiting of the Camelot government in exile." His favorite student was Hillary Rodham. He had no difficulty getting Rodino and Doar to hire Hillary.

In a temporary office in the former Congressional Hotel, Hillary became a liaison between Marshall at Yale and Doar in Washington. She also worked under the supervision of Bernard Nussbaum, Doar's Senior Associate Counsel. Like Doar and Marshall, Nussbaum had also served in the Kennedy Justice Department.

Marshall, Doar, Nussbaum, and Hillary all shared personal ambitions in helping Ted Kennedy to win the White House in 1976. Their goal was to keep Nixon "twisting in the wind" in office for as long as possible. This would prevent Vice President Jerry Ford from replacing Nixon and restoring the Republican Party's credibility.

They also feared that in his defense Nixon might assert that the Watergate burglary was carried out to protect national security. He could argue that as a precedent, and also in the name of national security, John Kennedy had engaged in assassination efforts against Fidel Castro with the aid of Mafia boss Sam Giancana. (Years later this and other misdeeds were to be documented in the reports of the Senate's "Church" Committee on Intelligence.)

Under Marshall's guidance Hillary drafted a series of changes to the House of Representatives' traditional rules—changes that were calculated both to delay the proceedings and avoid disclosure of President Kennedy's misdeeds. The first of these would have denied President Nixon representation by counsel. After prolonged debates this and other proposed rule changes were eventually voted down by a bipartisan coalition of Democrats and Republicans.

In addition, Hillary was assigned to confer with a group of Yale professors and obtain their imprimatur on a sanitized history of John Kennedy and other prior presidents. This was kept secret from the members of the Judiciary Committee and was to be used only if necessary to counter Nixon's anticipated defense. Members of Congress did not learn about it until after Nixon resigned. It was then published commercially—which raised a still unanswered question as to whether Hillary was paid royalties.

PART ONE
The Nixon Impeachment

1

The New Chairman

On a cold January day in 1973 President Lyndon Johnson's body lay in state in the rotunda of the Capitol. As the line of mourners filed by his casket, another ritual was taking place in the chamber of the House of Representatives. As it did at the beginning of each new Congress, the House was electing the chairs of its standing committees. In keeping with the seniority system, House members automatically cast their votes for Peter Rodino of Newark, New Jersey to be the new chairman of the Judiciary Committee.

Baptized as "Pelligrino Rodino" (later anglicized to Peter Wallace Rodino, Jr.) Peter had grown up in a roach-infested apartment over a slum candy store. When he was five years old his mother died of tuberculosis. With his father at work in a Newark leather factory, Rodino grew up on the streets of Newark's Little Italy.

With his hard-working father as a role model Rodino excelled in high school and then worked his way through college and law school by taking such jobs as railroad laborer, insurance salesman, factory hand, and social worker. During World War II he enlisted in the army, received a commission as a captain and served in a unit that helped liberate Italy. Returning home to New Jersey he won election to Congress in 1948—unseating Republican Fred Hartley, co-author of what Rodino described as the "iniquitous anti-labor Taft-Hartley Act."

When he became our chairman Rodino was in his sixties, his thick black hair already well-silvered. A short man, he wore elevator shoes. He was trim and impeccably dressed, usually wearing a well-tailored pinstriped suit and an elegant Italian silk tie. On his lapel was a small silk insignia attesting to his membership in the Knights of Malta, a centuries-old secret Catholic society.

Now at the height of his political power, Rodino faced a crisis. Newark was no longer comprised mostly of Italian-Americans. A majority of its voters were now blacks. He feared he would be a one-term chairman of the Judiciary Committee.

By that time I had been with the committee for eleven years and was serving as chief counsel to our subcommittee on Civil Rights. When Rodino summoned me to his office to offer me my new job he gave me a handwritten note which he had headed "Hot Potatoes"—listing what he perceived as the most explosive political issues before the committee: abortion, the death penalty, crime, drugs, school prayer, and whether to make Martin Luther King's birthday a national holiday.

Fearful that a mishandling of any of these polarizing issues might endanger his chances of re-election, he made it clear that my role would be to juggle the hot potatoes and help shield him from their heat. Ironically, although revelations about the break-in of the Watergate offices of Democratic National Committee were coming out rapidly in the Washington Post, the scandal was conspicuously absent from the list.

Rodino and I often dined together after work in an Italian restaurant. There he occasionally talked about a famous opera diva, Maria Jeritza—who was one of his constituents and a close friend. Her most famous role was as Salome', who enticed Herod to bring her the head of John the Baptist on a platter. On the day that Rodino became our chairman neither of us could have predicted that in the near future an aged Maria Jeritza, her eyes still lustrous with mischief, would teasingly suggest that he bring her the head of Richard Nixon.

2

Cancer on the Presidency

The one person at the Nixon White House whom both Rodino and I knew and understood best was Nixon's 30 year old chief counsel, John Wesley Dean III. In the early 1960s Dean had been my Republican counterpart on our Minority Staff. At that time he worked under the supervision of Republican Congressman Bill McCullough of Ohio, who had supported the civil rights acts that we had processed during the Johnson administration.

On April 17, 1973 we were dismayed when the Washington Post devoted half of its entire front page—the most space yet to a Watergate story—to an article targeting Dean as a felon, stating: "Former Attorney General John Mitchell and White House Counsel John W. Dean III approved and helped plan the Watergate bugging operation, according to President Nixon's former Special Assistant, Jeb Stuart Magruder. Mitchell and Dean later arranged to buy the silence of the seven convicted Watergate conspirators."

In June, Dean was subpoenaed by Senator Ervin's Watergate Committee to tell what he knew about the Watergate cover-up. Recalling dates and events in meticulous detail, Dean described a "cancer on the presidency." He said that the Nixon White House had "lost its moral compass." He admitted his own role in the cover-up, but attributed the whole plan to Nixon—whom Dean said had personally ordered him to "keep his fingers in the holes" and pay hush money to Howard Hunt and the other burglars.

The next morning, Tip O'Neill joined Rodino and me for breakfast. He said: "Dean refuses to be the fall guy. My guess is that in fingering Nixon, he's telling the truth. Hey, Nixon ran the dirtiest campaign in my lifetime.

He talks out of both sides of his mouth, whistles through the middle. He's a liar. What do you think?"

Having known Dean for ten years, I said, "Dean would never have stuck his neck out to cover up Watergate without enough authority from Nixon to be sure that Nixon would give him the credit."

If Dean had committed a felony under Nixon's orders, then under the United States Criminal Code the President himself was a co-conspirator and a felon. O'Neill said: "Impeachment is going to hit this Congress and we'd better be ready for it!" Rodino agreed to let me start discreetly preparing for impeachment, "just in case."

3

Secret Tapes, Deep Throat, and the CIA

In 1973 the thirteenth of July fell on a Friday. It was an ill-fated day for President Nixon. On that day Senate investigators learned that he had been secretly taping his conversations in the Oval Office. The revelation sent shock waves on Capitol Hill among those Democrats and Republicans who had previously had confidential conversations involving political deals with Nixon. Also, if investigators could get their hands on a tape that corroborated John Dean's testimony, the President's guilt for conspiring to obstruct justice could be proved beyond a doubt.

By having his conversations taped, Nixon may well have been the architect of his own downfall. But his fall from political grace must also be credited in part to the Washington Post and its reporter Robert Woodward—and from their secret source, whom they nicknamed "Deep Throat." Sensational revelations attributed to Deep Throat were eventually published by Woodward and Carl Bernstein in their book *All the President's Men.*

We later learned that Howard Hunt, who headed the Watergate burglars, had first been employed by the CIA during the Eisenhower administration. He later played a key role in the efforts of the Kennedy administration and the mob to assassinate Castro.

In 1971 following the leaking to the New York Times of the secret firebombing of Cambodia, Hunt was transferred to the White House to head "the plumbers." Their role was to ferret out anyone in the government who was leaking sensitive information to the press.

Under Hunt's leadership the group committed a number of illegal break-ins and wiretaps of persons whose names were on the White House "enemies list." These included Daniel Ellsberg who had leaked the Vietnam War's secret "Pentagon Papers" to the New York Times. The first assignment for Hunt and the plumbers was to break into the office of Ellsberg's psychiatrist in search of files embarrassing to Ellsberg.

Later assignments included break-ins of embassies, wiretaps of journalists, and the electronic bugging of offices of government officials who were suspected of leaking information—including Henry Kissinger's assistant Morton Halperin. In 1970 the Plumbers also committed crimes under the direction of the Committee for the Re-Election of President Nixon.

On June 17, 1972, Hunt and four others were surprised by a policeman in the act of rifling and wiretapping the office of the Democratic National Committee at the Watergate apartment and office complex. Dressed in suits and ties, with their hands in gloves and their pockets filled with sequentially numbered $100 bills, they were searched, arrested and booked for burglary.

After Hunt's arrest for the Watergate burglary his White House safe was opened by John Dean and its contents burned by FBI director Patrick Gray. Nixon also ordered Dean to pay money to Howard Hunt and other burglars to obtain their silence.

4

The Ford Confirmation and the Firing of Cox

In October 1973 Vice-President Spiro Agnew was under indictment for accepting bribes from his prior days as governor of Maryland. On October 10 he entered into a plea bargain with the U.S. Attorney, resigned his office, paid a small fine, and stayed out of jail. To replace him President Nixon nominated House Minority Leader Gerald Ford to be our new Vice President.

Highly respected on both sides of the political aisle Ford had been a member of the House of Representatives for 24 years He enjoyed the support of Speaker Carl Albert and Majority Leader Tip O'Neill as well as the Republicans. When his confirmation was referred to our committee it seemed certain that there would be no trouble.

We had just started work on the Ford confirmation when another major crisis arose. On October 20, vexed by Watergate Special Prosecutor Archibald Cox's subpoenas for his White House tapes, the President had ordered Attorney General Richardson to fire Cox or resign. Richardson resigned. William Ruckelshaus, now acting Attorney General, also refused to fire Cox, and was sacked by Nixon. Solicitor General Robert Bork was next in line—and fired Cox. The media called it the "Saturday Night Massacre."

Until then Rodino had successfully resisted consideration of Nixon's impeachment in our Committee. But events forced his hand. Eighty-four members of Congress introduced impeachment resolutions. Speaker Carl Albert referred them to us.

On the day of the referral Tip O'Neill sat beside us in the House chamber—pressing us to expedite Ford's confirmation and then impeach

Nixon as soon as possible. This was not what Rodino wanted to hear. He replied "Get the hell off my back!"

At least a foot taller and a hundred pounds heavier than Rodino, Tip rose from his chair and placed a large hand on Rodino's shoulder. "Look!" he said, "You've got one guy on your back. But I've got two hundred and forty guys on *mine*!" Knowing that O'Neill had discretion to provide campaign contributions to Democratic members of his own choosing, Rodino reluctantly agreed to move on impeachment.

When I awoke the next morning the news seemed unreal. Nixon had declared a military alert, putting U.S. air, ground, and naval forces worldwide in a state of combat readiness because of a supposed crisis in the Middle East. At breakfast in the House dining room, Tip O'Neill, Jack Brooks, and I feared the alert was a counteroffensive against the House Democrats in the media war that Watergate had become. The frightening thought also arose that Nixon might be irrational; if so, Congress had to act promptly to challenge this abuse of the presidency's considerable powers. Because of the extraordinary events of that time, with Rodino's encouragement I began to tape a personal diary of the impeachment in the privacy of my home. My first entry was on November 12, 1973:

This evening Rodino told me about a conversation he had with columnist Jack Anderson. According to Anderson there is a scheme afoot in the Department of Justice to engage in a criminal investigation of Rodino. Needless to say, this gives me much food for thought. There is a question as to whether the United States will be the kind of country in which I want to live if Richard Nixon is not removed from the White House.

When I left Rodino tonight I expressed this view to him. He spoke in favor of an "objective inquiry" and also expressed misgivings about the ability of Congress to cope with impeachment.

The Judiciary Committee Democrats were split on impeachment. Some far left committee members, nicknamed the "fire-eaters," defied our party leaders, Tip O'Neill and Speaker Albert. They denounced Ford as a "racist" and opposed his confirmation. Much as they publicly excoriated Nixon, at our closed-door meetings they argued in favor of prolonging the impeachment proceedings for partisan gains.

The principal *fire-eaters* included Charlie Rangel (D-NY), Father Robert Drinan (D-Ma), and Elizabeth Holtzman (D-NY) At the time Rangel was a freshman who had made a name for himself in Harlem by discrediting Reverend Adam Clayton Powell, the first black congressman since reconstruction. (In 1997 within an hour after New York Senator Moynihan announced his retirement Rangel was to phone Hillary Clinton and was the first to persuade her to run for the Senate in New York.)

Drinan was a Jesuit priest who was so strident and so unremitting in his public denunciation of Nixon that the media nicknamed him "The Mad Monk." He was eventually given an ultimatum by the Pope to get out of politics or get out of the Jesuit order. He then retired to a Jesuit law school. Holtzman was by nature so abrasive that her own staff nicknamed her "Ms Brillo-Pad."

In contrast to the *fire-eaters* Jack Brooks (D-Tex) was Tip O'Neill's staunchest supporter on the committee. His public and private personas differed sharply. Privately he was a man of intense sensitivity who feared being bruised by close contact with other politicians. Publicly, Jack was the archetypical Texas lawman. Journalist Howard Fields saw him this way:

"Brooks was a cigar-chomping, fast-talking Texan, who liked to use whatever power he had and liked cracking heads. He was gregarious and his humor and language were salty . . . . Jack Brooks would have voted to impeach Nixon if the vote were taken the day after Nixon was first inaugurated. It wouldn't look good to have done it on the same day, Brooks might have said; 'Let the son of a bitch have one good day.'

November 13: I picked Rodino up and drove him to the Capitol this morning for a breakfast meeting with our Judiciary Committee Democrats.

Don Edwards (D-Ca) was the principal spokesman. Since Nixon has announced that he will turn over the tapes, Don said "the steam is out of the impeachment movement." He expressed the thought that we would probably not be able to impeach Nixon—and it would be very good for the Democratic members who were running in the next election to be able to run against Nixon. I feel that there is too much sentiment of that sort among the fire-eaters, who want Nixon to twist in the wind.

Privately, I said to Don: "The question is: What kind of a country are we going to have if Nixon is not removed from office?" I feel strongly about this. Nixon has put Congress to a test.

The enjoyable part of the meeting was my conversations sitting between Brooks and Rodino. Jack said, "You and Pete better start eating plenty of raw meat for breakfast—or the Republicans will screw us."

To assure the privacy of the caucus, we often met in a hideaway office behind the House dining room known as the "Board of Education Room." During the Prohibition Era, the beautifully furnished room was used by

Speaker Nicholas Longworth for drinking parties with other House members. (The hideaway's name originally came from what Longworth learned after plying his guests with bourbon.)

Like Longworth, Rodino mostly played the role of a good listener. Jack Brooks tended to play the role of our reticent chairman's executive officer. I tried to be a navigator—to take political and legal bearings and occasionally recommend changes in speed and direction.

November 14: There was a rancorous meeting of the Democratic members this morning in the Board Room. It went on and off all day long. Essentially the theme was the same—the far left wingers oppose Ford's confirmation.

Rangel, Father Drinan and Elizabeth Holtzman were rancorous about not even allowing the confirmation to be put to a vote. When I tried gently to suggest that the Twenty-fifth Amendment might give us a constitutional duty to at least have a vote on the question of Ford's qualifications, Rangel laughed and Holtzman scoffed

Rodino took a strong position—stronger than I've ever seen him take. He told Rangel, Drinan and Holtzman : "You can take all the political positions you want. As for me I will not be guided by you, but by my conscience."

In the middle of the meeting Jack Brooks tried to calm down the meeting by mentioning that on the very spot where Bob Kastenmeier was sitting, Harry Truman had once sat drinking bourbon with House Speaker Sam Rayburn—and had received a call from Eleanor Roosevelt telling him that President Roosevelt had just died. I don't think this made the slightest impression on Rangel—who couldn't care less

November 15: Before the Ford hearings began this morning, Rodino and I had breakfast with Tip O'Neill. We told him about the flack we were getting from Rangel, Drinan and Holtzman. O'Neill seemed sympathetic and quite surprised. He said he would do his best to keep them in line.

With the media present, the hearings began promptly at 10 a.m. I think they went well. Most of the members were not such firebrands when having to face the TV cameras.

Tonight I continue to feel jaded. When I count heads on the Judiciary Committee on both sides of the aisles, the men of good will and decency are the exception and not the rule. Hutchinson [the Judiciary Committee's ranking Republican] is a pro-Nixon conservative, yet he is decent, with integrity, and a man of good will. For me, the people of good will also include Democrats Ray Thornton of Arkansas and Barbara Jordan of Texas.

I enjoyed Jack Brooks during the debate on the House floor: all piss and vinegar, but at least with balls. If he doesn't always have good will, at least he has integrity and balls.

Among facts that were not widely publicized in the media we learned that several years earlier Ford had consultations with a psychiatrist who had also treated Nixon. We also learned that although Ford was a conservative Republican, his wife, Betty, who had been a member of the Martha Graham Dance Company, was a "closet liberal" and supported ERA, feminism, and abortion rights—and became an alcoholic.

In those years, the public disclosure by a congressional committee of such personal matters was considered inappropriate—even by most of the *fire-eaters*.

November 20: Every head count in the House and Senate predicted that Ford would soon be confirmed. The Senate Committee on Rules and Administration unanimously approved his nomination.

November 21: The Ford hearings began again at 11 a.m. Although it is the day before Thanksgiving the hearing lasted for most of the day—with testimony from Ford. I avoided the hearings and tried to continue work on putting together the impeachment inquiry.

November 26: We held the last confirmation hearing today with an additional three-and-one-half hours of cross-examination of Ford. The truth is that no one has really laid a glove on Ford in terms of demonstrating any form of corruption or criminality.

November 27: In the afternoon, the Senate voted to confirm Ford 92 to 3. Three Democrats voted against Ford: Eagleton of Missouri, Hathaway of Maine, and Gaylord Nelson of Wisconsin.

November 28: Rodino called me at 7 a.m. He is afraid that if he votes to confirm Ford, the blacks and liberals in his district will be inflamed by Charlie Rangel and the Congressional Black Caucus

Later in the day we talked further about it. He said he had spoken to Ford privately and had told him that he would help get the confirmation out of committee and onto the floor, but that he might have to vote against him during the recorded votes on the floor. He said that Ford was very understanding and thanked him for his handling of the whole situation in the committee.

November 29: Rodino and a majority of the committee voted to confirm Ford. The meeting went well. The members behaved themselves fairly well except for Holtzman, who was sanctimonious and tried to prevent the issue from even being brought to a vote. She brought a formal motion to table the confirmation, then insisted stridently that the committee debate her motion. Even though Rodino advised her gently that under House rules motions to table are not debatable, she started shouting. Rodino had to gavel her down.

Rodino handled the meeting extremely well. If anything, he was perhaps a bit too relaxed.

Jack Brooks was in a good mood, saying of Ford: "I don't think Vice President is good enough for him. I hope we can promote him as quickly as possible."

November 30: Because of fear of retribution by Rangel and the Congressional Black Caucus Rodino is still trying to decide how to vote on the Ford confirmation when it comes up on the floor. He still wants to vote "No." December 6: Tonight Rodino and I went to the House floor for the debate on the Ford confirmation and the swearing-in ceremony. Tonight I am trying to rest, listening to the following radio newscast: "Gerald Ford was confirmed as the Vice President of the United States by the House of Representatives this afternoon by a vote of 387 to 35. Ford was sworn into office about 90 minutes later during a joint meeting of the Congress as his wife and the President stood beside him. There was never any question about the Ford confirmation, only how soon it would come and how extensive the opposition . . . . In the House, the "no" votes totaled 35, all from California, New York, and Massachusetts. Ten of the 16 black members of the House opposed Gerald Ford."

Later, Victor Lasky, author of *It Didn't Start With Watergate* was to write: "When Ford's name was finally placed in nomination, Rodino remarked that never before had any man undergone such an investigation and emerged so well. So what did Rodino do? He voted against confirmation."

5

Impeachment Begins

By the time Ford was confirmed officers of 111 AFL-CIO international unions, representing more than 14 million members, had come to Capitol Hill to lobby for impeachment.

All the President's Men became a best-selling book and a box-office hit. Under the aegis of the Washington Post's publisher, Katherine Graham, "Deep Throat" had acquired respectability as a "reliable source." On Pennsylvania Avenue, "Honk for Impeachment" became Washington's best-selling bumper sticker.

That Nixon's impeachment had become viable was clear to Tip O'Neill. He had engaged William Hamilton, a pioneer in political polling, to take soundings in each of the 435 congressional districts. Among Democrats only 7 percent would vote for any candidate who opposed impeachment.

O'Neill was getting plenty of feed back from House Democrats. In a quote from his biography, he said: "On the Monday after Congress returned from the Thanksgiving recess, I spent the entire morning hearing what I call 'confessions' as the members came to me with their problems and their reports from home. I must have had sixty or seventy guys come up to condemn the Judiciary Committee for dragging its feet. When they went back to their districts the members were starting to look stupid because they didn't know what was going on in the Judiciary Committee."

When Tip asked me what was going on I explained that Charlie Rangel and the left wing *fire-eaters* were polarizing the Democrats and keeping our committee in turmoil. They ranted mostly about two questions: whether we should hire a "big name" lawyer to head the impeachment inquiry staff; and which committee members Rodino should appoint to have overall supervision of the staff's investigation. As a freshman Rangel had also published an article in the New York Times chastising Rodino for considering the use of a seniority system in committee appointments.

November 26: Rodino and I met again tonight in his office and discussed the special counsel problem While I was there he spoke for about a half hour with Sargent Shriver (Ted Kennedy's brother in law), who is promoting Ted Kennedy for President in 1976 and recommended that we hire John Doar, a former Assistant Attorney General, to head our impeachment inquiry staff.

During the day Nixon's secretary Rose Mary Woods testified before the Senate Watergate Committee today that she pushed the wrong button or something and created an eighteen-minute gap in one of the subpoenaed White House tapes.

This afternoon I had an extraordinary experience. Rodino had asked me to call Clark Clifford (the former Secretary of Defense) *and give him the list of the names of lawyers under consideration for the job of special counsel. I called him and he asked me to come to his office at 4 o'clock. He has a palatial office with a beautiful view looking down over the White House. When I arrived he apologized for asking me to come there, and explained that he will not speak freely on the phone or in government offices because of the possibility of illegal wiretaps and bugging devices. Amazing!*

Then Clifford proceeded to pontificate a bit. He gave me a twenty-minute lecture on Nixon. I was annoyed that he felt the need to lecture me on why Nixon should be impeached. He went through the whole bit—from Helen Gahagan Douglas to Jerry Voorhis—the picture of Nixon as a "ruthless character assassin" with a political philosophy that is "totalitarian" and "antithetical to our way of life." The one thing that Clifford contributed to my thinking about Nixon was his heavy emphasis on Nixon's personal finances. For example, he talked with some knowledge about Nixon's lots in Key Biscayne.

Regarding the choice of a special impeachment counsel Clifford advised me not to be impressed at all with big names. He said, "Most big names are simply people who have good public relations staffs." He also had a reservation about John Doar, because of Doar's close ties to Burke Marshall, Ted Kennedy's chief political strategist,

December 4: My afternoon was hectic. Capitol Hill has become a jungle in which most of the tigers are made out of paper—but where the administrative problems can kill you—, like vicious, swarming mosquitoes that can eat you alive. I went home thinking that I would really prefer a job at half the salary on the impeachment inquiry staff working on a single project that I can get my teeth into and master.

December 6: Rodino and I had a breakfast meeting with some of the junior Democrats: Waldie, Seiberling, Holtzman, Owens, Mezvinsky, and of course Charlie Rangel. Like Rangel they are worried that they will not get a fair share of press coverage from the impeachment proceedings.

Rangel and the other far left Democrats approach the problem entirely from a self-serving partisan point of view. There was no discussion of how best to conduct a vigorous and effective investigation of the President or of the responsibility of committee members to supervise such an investigation.

Tonight in my car on the way home from the Capitol, Rodino and I discussed our vexing day. We were both shocked by how self serving such Democrats as Rangel and Holtzman are.

By this time, more than two months had passed since the impeachment resolutions had been referred to the committee and we began our search for a special counsel. I and our staff were limited by Rodino to studying documents obtained from other committees. We were not even allowed to interview any potential witnesses.

A leading news magazine described our committee as *The Tortoise on the Hill*. In addition some of the many impatient impeachment proponents in the House were considering introducing a privileged resolution—a parliamentary device to debate and vote on impeachment without waiting for recommendations from the Judiciary Committee.

Throughout this period Senator Ted Kennedy and Yale professor Burke Marshall were pressing Rodino to appoint John Doar as our special impeachment counsel. Doar had been Marshall's deputy in President John Kennedy's Justice Department. On December 16 Rodino finally decided on Doar.

6

John Doar

On his first day on our Committee payroll Doar requested permission from Rodino to confer privately on impeachment matters with Burke Marshall, his former boss in the Kennedy Justice Department. I objected and reminded Rodino and Doar that it would be a violation of House and Committee rules for a staff counsel to disclose confidential committee business. Rodino then told Doar, "If you do it, you will have to be very discreet about it."

One of the first lawyers to be hired by Doar was Marshall's star pupil Hillary Rodham. Our staff office manager was later to learn from Hillary's telephone logs that she was in touch with Marshall daily

It was not until after Nixon's resignation that a book titled *How the Good Guys Finally Won,* by New York journalist Jimmy Breslin, tried to explain and justify Doar's strategy, stating: "Doar had made two major decisions about how the case should be conducted. He decided not to do any investigating of his own, but to simply pick up the materials gathered by the Ervin Committee and the Special Prosecutor's office and work from there. He thought that an investigation, interrogating witnesses on television, would give the public the idea that everybody was doing the same thing over and over and the entire idea of impeachment might lose its effect."

Breslin, who had recently arrived on Capitol Hill either ignored or was unaware of the fact that the Ervin Committee's authority had been expressly limited by an amendment offered by Ted Kennedy to preclude the committee from investigating presidential misconduct. Also Special Watergate Prosecutor Archibald Cox (who had been Solicitor General during the Kennedy presidency) decided to exercise "prosecutorial discretion" to intentionally avoid investigating Nixon.

In the winter of 1973, Doar confided only in such key staff aides as Hillary Rodham and Nussbaum that in the Kennedy administration the Justice Department had conducted illegal wiretaps as well as black-bag burglaries and a variety of political surveillance programs—and that it would be impolitic for him now to investigate the Nixon's perpetuation of such government-sponsored crimes.

It was not until 1975—after Nixon had resigned and Ford was President—that Doar's own unlawful surveillance activities were first to become public. A commission headed by Vice President Nelson Rockefeller was established by President Ford to investigate the CIA. Although the media took little notice, the commission's report revealed that, as Assistant Attorney General for Civil Rights in 1967, Doar had recommended the establishment of "a single intelligence unit to analyze the FBI information we receive about persons who make the urban ghetto their base of operations."

In approving Doar's recommendations, Attorney General Ramsey Clark had cautioned Doar and other assistant attorneys general that "the planning and creation of the unit must be kept in strictest confidence." (In later years Ramsey Clark was to become nationally discredited for his defense of the authoritarian War Crimes of Slobodon Molosevic and Saddam Hussein.)

As the Rockefeller Commission Report of 1975 further noted: "The FBI was to constitute only one source of information for the proposed unit. As additional sources Doar suggested federal poverty programs, Labor Department programs, and neighborhood legal services. Doar recognized the 'sensitivity' of using such additional sources, but nevertheless thought these sources would have access to relevant facts. Other sources of dissident information suggested by Doar included the Intelligence Unit of the Internal Revenue Service and perhaps the Post Office Department."

Several years later, journalist Victor Lasky described both Rodino and John Doar as being in league with Harvard Professor Arthur Schlesinger—who had been the historian in residence in the Kennedy White House and later authored *The Imperial Presidency*, a critique of the Nixon administration. Lasky wrote:

"In Congress many years before coming to public notice, Rodino had never expected to be courted by the likes of Schlesinger, one of the nation's more publicized intellectuals. And in all probability Schlesinger had never expected to be courting the likes of Rodino, a product of the Essex County Democratic Organization.

"But the stakes were high. One of [Schlesinger's] pals from Camelot days now actually running the impeachment inquiry was none other than John Doar, formerly head of the Civil Rights Division in Robert Kennedy's Justice Department. This of course was the same Doar who, when informed of the FBI's campaign to denigrate Martin Luther King, had done nothing to stop it.

"It was the same Doar who had urged Attorney General Clark in 1967 to seek intelligence information from government workers in the nation's black communities. Doar's memorandum, written September 27, 1967, following the Detroit riots, led to the creation of a computerized intelligence file that eventually grew to contain some 18,000 names, mainly of black militants. This was the kind of activity which Doar and others on the impeachment panel had sought to characterize as 'abuses of power' under Nixon.

"Later as president of the New York City Board of Education Doar did a switch. He catered to the black militants, refusing for example to dismiss extremist teachers who made anti-Semitic remarks in class. Arnold Forster and Benjamin R. Epstein of the Anti-Defamation League pointed out that "when William O. Marley, chairman of the Brownsville Model Cities Committee, in a long anti-Semitic diatribe, repeatedly attacked Jews as dominant in the school system there was no challenge from President Doar."

Along with Burke Marshall, John Doar became another role model for Hillary Rodham.

7

Hillary and Her Role Models

Twenty years after Watergate in *Hillary Clinton: The Inside Story*, Hillary's official authorized biographer, Judith Warner, noted that, when Hillary joined the impeachment inquiry staff at the age of twenty-six, "the fact that she'd been chosen by civil rights giant Burke Marshall gave her added clout." The biography also noted that "that there was considerable tension between Hillary's group and the permanent staff of the House Judiciary Committee."

As described in her biography: "Hillary's main assignment was establishing the legal procedures to be followed . . . It meant staying in the background and being above all discreet."

In 1974, I had discussions with Hillary on a number of occasions. After she was hired, one of the first covert assignments that Doar and Nussbaum gave her was to prepare confidential drafts of impeachment procedures recommended by Marshall.

After Hillary completed some early drafts, Nussbaum instructed her to consult me for clarification of the current rules—but not to disclose that Marshall had already recommended changes. When I asked Hillary if she or anyone else on the inquiry staff had prepared any drafts of impeachment procedures, she said "No."

A month before Doar, Nussbaum, and Rodham had been hired we had published an official codification of the existing impeachment procedures—many of which had been in effect since the days of Thomas Jefferson. We had also sent a copy to every member of the House of Representatives.

At my first meeting with Hillary I gave her several copies of our impeachment rules. I also explained that at a meeting that Rodino and I had with Speaker Albert, Majority Leader Tip O'Neill and Parliamentarian Lou Deschler we all agreed not to change any of the rules. Tip O'Neill had put it this way : "To try to change the rules would be like changing the rules of baseball just before a World Series. It would generate a national debate on the fairness of the new rules, and polarize the Congress. It would also make it more difficult to get votes to impeach the President."

A few days later, Hillary consulted me again as to whether President Nixon had a right to be represented by counsel at any evidentiary hearings. My response was: "Yes, of course the President should be represented by counsel. In fact, the committee specifically considered the counsel question just a few years ago during our recent impeachment inquiry regarding Justice Douglas. From the very beginning of the proceedings we allowed Douglas to be represented by Simon Rifkind, a former federal judge."

After her consultation with me Hillary Rodham and John Doar obtained permission from Rodino to transfer our supply of impeachment rules from our usual storeroom to the offices of the Impeachment Inquiry Staff in their exclusive custody. They also transferred all of our Douglas impeachment files. Thus our impeachment procedure books and our Douglas files were no longer available to the public.

My first outright clash with Rodham, Doar and Nussbaum occurred as the result of a legal memorandum written by Hillary arguing that President Nixon not be allowed representation by counsel.

House Speaker Carl Albert, House Parliamentarian Lou Deschler, and Majority Leader Tip O'Neill, and I were dismayed by the memorandum. Not only did we regard Hillary's position as unethical, but we feared that if we denied Nixon representation by counsel we might not have enough votes to impeach him. (In short, many members who ordinarily would vote "Yes" would oppose any articles of impeachment adopted under unconstitutional procedures.)

Rodino at first supported Hillary's recommendation. When I told him that if Nixon were denied representation by counsel I would resign in protest, he equivocated and assumed a posture above the fray. At the same time, Charlie Rangel, the *fire-eater* far left wing of the committee, and most members of the Congressional Black Caucus championed Hillary's divisive memorandum.

At first the only Democratic Congressman who publicly opposed Hillary's memorandum was Jack Brooks (D-Tex). After weeks of wrangling with the *fire-eaters* Jack lost his temper and told them "I don't give a damn about your candy—assed partisan strategies. I want to be able to look my grandchildren in the eye."

After that Don Edwards (who had a reputation as the Committee's most "flaming" liberal) joined with Brooks. The moderate Democrats also joined with them. When it then became clear that Brooks and Edwards combined with the Republicans had the votes, Rodino finally agreed to allow attorney James St. Clair to have the same rights to represent Nixon that we had given to the attorney in our Douglas impeachment proceedings.

Undaunted by their defeat of their scheme to deny Nixon representation by counsel, Marshall and Rodham concocted an even more invidious scheme. Hillary drafted a resolution that created a firewall between the Impeachment Inquiry Staff and all of the members of the Committee with the exception of Rodino and the ranking minority member, Ed Hutchinson (R-Mich). It instructed Doar and his staff not to disclose their findings to the Committee or to anyone in the media until their investigation of Nixon was completed.

Ironically, the resolution as drafted by Hillary was publicized as a means of "keeping partisan politics out of impeachment." As such it had the support of a majority of the committee members and was adopted.

Marshall, Doar, Nussbaum and Rodham also contemplated that there would be no hearings of live witnesses who could be cross examined by committee members. They also wanted the drafting of any proposed articles of impeachment be left solely to the Impeachment Inquiry Staff—with members of congress not allowed to offer amendments

In the end every one of the other Hillary drafted procedural rules were to be opposed not only by Brooks and Edwards but by Tip O'Neill and a majority of the Democrats in the House of Representatives.

8

The Strategy of Delay

On the morning of May 9, a long line of spectators stretched outside of Room 2141 of the Rayburn Building. Inside, a mob of reporters and TV cameramen milled about. When Rodino arrived, the klieg lights went on. Rodino sat in his leather chairman's chair, pounded his gavel to convene the hearing, and then entertained a motion to close the hearing. The motion was passed, the klieg lights went off, and the room was cleared of spectators and newsmen. The doors were locked, the hearing room was swept for electronic bugs, and the hearings began in "executive session."

To the disappointment of the networks and the public, the mahogany doors of Room 2141 remained locked and the proceedings secret for the next six weeks. During that period, no live witnesses were called and no testimony, sworn or otherwise, was heard from anyone other than Doar or his staff.

The "testimony" consisted of the inquiry staff simply reading aloud from photocopies of documents obtained by the Ervin Committee, the Watergate Special Prosecutor, and other bodies that had not conducted an impeachment investigation. At the end of the six weeks, the documents were published and released to the media en masse in the form of thirty-six volumes.

It was generally conceded by even the pro-impeachment media that the volumes of documents did not make the case. As described by an Associated Press reporter, "The Judiciary Committee was blowing smoke."

Washington Post reporter William Greider wrote, "Even the most bullish Democrats conceded that their investigations did not produce a thundering consensus that Nixon should be removed from office, the kind of compelling evidence which would remove all doubts about the outcome." Investigative journalist Victor Lasky later wrote::

"The thirty-eight members of the Judiciary Committee sat behind closed doors and listened to Doar drone out evidence. What Doar and his staff were doing was pulling together a vast amount of material from numerous sources: the Senate Watergate Committee, the Joint Committee on Internal Revenue Taxation, the Internal Revenue Service, grand juries and other congressional fact-finding committees. All this information was compiled in thirty-six black loose-leaf notebooks. Which is why, in the end Doar earned the title pinned on him by a detractor, 'The World's Greatest Archivist.'

"Even Democratic members were appalled. 'If these meetings were ever televised, the country would impeach us,' said one [Jack Brooks]. 'This isn't an investigation, it's a compilation,' said another [Walter Flowers].' And the Republicans agreed. 'Damned dull,' said Robert McClory of Illinois . . . . Congressman McClory also put it this way, 'I kept waiting for the bombshell to appear, and it never appeared' Even Democrats agreed that not one piece of evidence had been produced—no 'hand in the cookie jar' or 'smoking gun'—which would show conclusively that the President was guilty of a crime, or at least a broader impeachable offense."

In 1976 an article titled *Searching for the Real Nixon Scandal* was published by Renata Adler who had been one of Doar's closest confidantes for several years prior to his putting her on our payroll. Adler's contention was that the non-investigation orchestrated by Doar was a "valuable charade" in that it allowed Doar and a smaller group that included Hillary and Nussbaum to do the important work. As Adler described the non-investigation: "The machine itself, firmly required to be directionless, produced, naturally enough, no investigation, and in the end no case. It is commonly said that 'the case' is in those thirty-odd staff volumes. Only by people who have not read them: hardly anyone has read them."

In response to the strategy of delay Nixon charged the Democrats with "Wallowing in Watergate." The Republican slogan became "Impeach him or get off his back!" Vice-President Ford wrote: "A relatively small group of political activists tried to cripple the President by dragging out the impeachment preliminaries for as long as they could and use the affair for maximum political advantage."

Later in his autobiography *Man of the House*, Tip O'Neill also discussed the strategy of delay, stating: "On more than one occasion I had to light a fire under Rodino's feet. I told him 'You also have to keep it from becoming political.' It was extremely important to keep the impeachment hearings from deteriorating into partisan warfare. After all, the longer Richard Nixon remained in office the more we would gain. Had the President stayed on through the 1974 congressional elections, we would have picked up even more seats than we did. And if Nixon had served out his full second term, the 1976 presidential election would have been a foregone conclusion."

9

Thrusting Greatness on Rodino

In the Democratic cloakroom, Brooks often articulated his impeachment strategy in Shakespearean as well as biblical terms, saying: "We shouldn't disgrace Pete unless we have to. We should thrust greatness upon him." He also quoted Jeremiah: "Cursed be he who doeth the work of the Lord with a slack hand. And cursed be he who keepeth his sword back from blood."

It was not only Democrats who were clamoring for impeachment. Robert Welch, founder of the ultraconservative John Birch Society, had characterized Nixon as "the most disingenuous and slipperiest politician that ever showed up on the American scene."

When a delegation of fundamentalist clergymen met with Senator Barry Goldwater, their spokesman said, "Senator, all of us know that Nixon is a liar! If he is not impeached, how can we teach the ten commandments in our Sunday schools?"

The Senator's son Congressman Barry Goldwater, Jr. was a very close friend of John and Maureen Dean. Father and son were confident that Dean was telling the truth and that Nixon was a liar. The Goldwaters also shared their views with their fellow Arizona Republican, Congressman John Rhodes—who had become Vice President Ford's successor as House minority leader.

Rhodes was now having daily private meetings with Tip O'Neill. He was persuaded that O'Neill was not in favor of partisan strategy of delay—and wasn't trying to keep Nixon twisting in the wind to assure electoral gains in 1976. Rhodes and O'Neill—like Brooks and Judicary Committee Republican

Bob McClory—were in agreement that the procedural rules drafted by Hillary under Burke Marshall's direction should be voted down.

It was agreed that we should hold hearings with live witnesses, including John Dean—and that contrary to Marshall's recommendation the members of the committee as well as Nixon's counsel should all have a right to cross examine Dean and the other witnesses.

This would give House Republicans such as McClory, who wanted to make impeachment bipartisan—the opportunity to vote "Yes." Above all, it would then give the House and Senate the opportunity to make Rhodes's mentor, Jerry Ford, President—and give Ford and Rhodes more than two years to restore confidence in the Republican party before the 1976 elections.

They also agreed that behind the scenes the control of the Judiciary Committee's impeachment should be given to Brooks in a way that avoided embarrassment to Rodino and allow him to appear to be still in charge.

Brooks and McClory were pleased—as was I. On a national level we regarded the compromise as a victory for non-partisanship. On a personal level we enjoyed Rodino's friendship for his affability and joviality. We also understood and had sympathy for his weaknesses. I for one was also particularly aware of his unswerving commitment to the Civil Rights Laws that we had enacted during the Johnson administration.

Under the new de facto leadership of Brooks and McCLory we scheduled hearings to start on July 2, 1974 with testimony of at least nine witnesses, the most crucial of whom were John Dean and his former boss, Attorney General John Mitchell. By then they like most of the other witness had committed felonies in the furtherance of Nixon's re-election campaign.

Before our hearings began, still unaware of the behind the-scenes change in our committee's leadership Doar pressed Rodino to bring up a Hillary-drafted resolution on the House floor to amend the traditional rules and prohibit committee members from interrogating witnesses—allowing cross examinations solely by Doar and Nixon's counsel.

Opposed by both the Democratic and Republican leadership of the House the resolution that Hillary had drafted was voted down. The defeat of the resolution was a turning point in the history of our proceedings. It was a signal to the entire Congress that Tip O'Neill and Jack Brooks now had control of our committee.

On the morning of July 11 Dean, guarded by U.S. Marshalls, and surrounded by a mob of reporters and cameramen, arrived at Room 2141 of the Rayburn building. He had been in the room countless times during the years he had served as the committee's minority counsel.

Nixon's counsel, James St. Clair, cross examined Dean meticulously for more than three hours. Dean's credibility was in effect corroborated by the testimony of former Attorney General John Mitchell who had recommend that Dean, at the age of 30, be appointed by Nixon to be Chief White House Counsel.

Later, after Nixon resigned, Watergate Prosecutor Leon Jaworski commented on St. Clair's cross-examination of Dean, stating: "St. Clair, while proclaiming the President innocent of wrongdoing to the committee, so far as I could ascertain had not made as much as a dent in the hard evidence."

On the conclusion of our evidentiary hearings we had at last established a record that was more than adequate to impeach President Nixon for felonies that Doar had obfuscated in his 38 volumes of documents.

Under the control of Tip O'Neill and Jack Brooks we then scheduled a televised debate on articles of impeachment to begin on Wednesday, July 24, 1974.

From Saturday, July 20, until after the televised hearings began on the night of July 24, members of two drafting groups from each party sequestered themselves from media coverage. First they considered the question of whether Nixon had in fact conspired with Dean and others to obstruct justice as alleged by Dean and charged by the Watergate grand jury. They agreed that the answer was "Yes."

Both drafting groups also took an "abuse of power" approach to impeachment. They concluded that, aside from the felony charge of obstruction of justice, Nixon should be impeached for violating his oath of office to defend the Constitution and faithfully execute the laws of the United States.

On July 24, the full Committee met at 7:30 p.m. to consider articles of impeachment For the first time in history, a congressional debate and roll call vote was recorded on television, and the coverage lasted until July 30. During that week, the committee adopted three articles of impeachment, all by fairly substantial bipartisan majorities.

Article I was the obstruction of justice felony charge. It passed on July 27 by a vote of 27 to 11.

Article II was based on abuse of constitutional powers and violations of the presidential oath, passed on July 29 by a vote of 28 to 10.

Article III charged the President with unlawfully refusing to comply fully with the committee's subpoenas. It was proposed by Bob McClory. Despite vigorous opposition from both Rodino and Doar, it passed on July 30 by a vote of 21 to 17.

After the articles of impeachment were adopted by the committee, Tip O'Neill scheduled a debate by the full House to begin in two weeks. The general mood in the House and throughout the country was that impeachment was a foregone conclusion.

But major questions persisted. Would Nixon resign? If not, how long would a Senate trial take? And if there was a Senate trial, would the Senate undertake the investigation that Rodino, Doar, Nussbaum, Rodham and Mashall had wanted to avoid?

10

The "Smoking Gun"

At 11 a.m. on July 24, 1974 the Supreme Court had met to announce their decision in *United States v. Nixon*. The case had been brought by Special Prosecutor Leon Jaworski to compel the President to turn over White House tapes that Nixon's counsel argued were shielded from disclosure by executive privilege.

Just two blocks away from the Rayburn Building—where the congressional drafting teams were feverishly preparing articles of impeachment—the traditional cry went out: "Oyez, Oyez, Oyez, God save the United States and this honorable court." Then Chief Justice Warren Burger, who had been appointed by President Nixon, announced that eight of the court's justices had ruled against the President and ordered him to turn over what the media soon called "the smoking gun tape."

On August 5, a transcript was released to the public. It showed that as early as three days after the break-in the President had personally directed Haldeman to press the CIA to instruct the FBI to turn off its investigation of the burglars in the interest of national security. Thus it corroborated Dean's incrimination of the President as a co-conspirator. As a result the Republicans on the Judiciary Committee who had previously voted "No" on impeachment changed their vote to "Aye."

On August 8, Nixon spoke to the nation on television at night, stating, "It has become evident to me that I no longer have a strong enough political base in the Congress . . . Therefore I shall resign the presidency effective at noon tomorrow."

On August 9 Jerry Ford was sworn in as President and in a brief inaugural address stated, "The long nightmare of Watergate is over." As the first non-elected President in our history he asked that the people "confirm me as your President in your prayers." With modesty he also added: "I am a Ford, not a Lincoln."

11

Hillary's Secret Book

In May 1977, Nixon made his first national appearance since his resignation in an interview with journalist David Frost, stating: "I did not commit, in my view, any impeachable offense . . . . I can only say that while technically I did not commit a crime, an impeachable offense . . . these are legalisms. As far as the handling of this [Watergate] matter is concerned, it was so botched-up. I made many bad judgments. The worst ones, mistakes of the heart rather than the head."

At one point in the interview, Nixon explained the basis of his defense: "When the president does it because of the national security that means that it is not illegal. If the president approves an action because of the national security, then the president's decision in that instance is one that enables those who carry it out to carry it out without violating a law. Otherwise, they're in an impossible position."

Did Doar know that Nixon had such a defense against a wide variety of charges of presidential misconduct? And did Doar, Nussbaum, Hillary, and Burke Marshall intentionally structure the impeachment inquiry to avoid the possibility of the assertion of such a defense? It was not until late September 1974, almost two months after Nixon's resignation, that it first became apparent to most of the members of the Committee—that the answer to both questions was "yes."

The revelation was provoked by a personal letter that Congressman Charles Wiggins sent to Rodino on September 26, 1974, stating that he had been disturbed to discover for the first time in an airport a publication titled; *Responses of Presidents to Charges of Misconduct Including Accusations of*

High Crimes and Misdemeanors from George Washington to Lyndon Johnson: An Authoritative History Requested by Counsel John Doar for the Impeachment Inquiry Staff Investigating Charges Against Richard M. Nixon.

In his letter Wiggins wrote: "It is requested that the facts concerning the matter be investigated and a report be made to the full committee as it concerns us all.

"Early last spring when it became obvious that the committee was considering presidential abuse of power as a possible ground of impeachment, I raised the question before the full committee that research should be undertaken so as to furnish a standard against which to test the alleged abusive conduct of Richard Nixon.

"As I recall, several other members joined with me in this request. I recall as well repeating this request from time to time during the course of our investigation. The [impeachment inquiry] staff, as I recall, was noncommittal, but it is certain that no such staff study was made available to the members at any time for their use.

"I am troubled especially by the possibility that information deemed essential by some of the members in their discharge of their responsibilities may have been intentionally suppressed by the staff during the course of our investigation. Also, we must resolve the question of whether the staff possesses a literary property right in nonpublic information collected during the course of our investigation."

On October 3, 1974 Rodino wrote a letter admitting that the report was received by Doar in July. To explain why it was kept secret he stated: "Hillary Rodham of the impeachment inquiry staff coordinated the work . . . The staff did not think the manuscript was useful in its present form."

In anticipation of the possibility that Nixon would assert such a defense Doar, Nussbaum and Burke Marshall had given Hillary a secret assignment that was not to be disclosed to the committee members even after the committee's self-imposed exclusion from access to the inquiry staff's confidential files was terminated.

Hillary had been assigned to work with Yale professor C. Vann Woodward—who was a colleague of Burke Marshall—to help him and a small group of Yale professors prepare a sanitized account of past abuses of presidential power that did not disclose the crimes committed during the Kennedy administration with the help of the Mafia.

Two years after Wiggins' letter to Rodino, Albert Jenner, Doar's Republican counterpart on the impeachment inquiry staff, was to say of the report, "We've kept it top secret. It was something we relied on very heavily."

Without the permission of Rodino and after Nixon's resignation the secret sanitized report was eventually published commercially.

For me as a cover-up of the crimes of the Kennedy administration Hillary's secret project had a pathetic irony—in that she had been hired to investigate Nixon's cover-up of Watergate. I also advised Rodino that as suggested in Wiggins' letter we should have investigated the question of whether Hillary or anyone else on the staff had asserted personal property rights in the document and received any royalties. (As far as I know no such investigation has ever taken place, either by Congress or a journalist.)

Shortly after that I resigned from the Judiciary Committee staff and took a teaching position at the University of Santa Clara in California.

PART TWO
The Clinton Presidency

12

Ascent to Power

Hillary was twenty-seven when the impeachment inquiry staff was disbanded. The next morning she took a train down to Little Rock, Arkansas. She moved in with Bill Clinton and they eventually married.

When Bill ran for Attorney General in 1977 his campaign was financed partly by the Riady family of Indonesia, which owned banks and had other investments in Arkansas. When he won the election Hillary became associated with the Rose law firm and brought the Riady enterprises with her as clients. The Riady's were to remain friends and financial backers of the Clinton for many years to come

In 1979 Bill became the nation's youngest governor and Hillary became a Rose partner. Thirteen years later in 1992, still financed in part by the Riady family, Bill campaigned for the Presidency. With Hillary alongside him in the hustings they promised "two for one" in high office.

Once in the White House Hillary became the first wife of a president to occupy a prominent office in the West Wing, with shared authority over the President's staff. A few days later her long time mentor Bernie Nussbaum was appointed chief White House counsel and moved into the office next to hers.

In the early weeks of the Clinton administration the White House had promised "the most ethical administration in history." It also announced the nomination of Patricia Wald, a highly respected federal judge to be attorney general. But the announcement was news to Judge Wald—who first learned about it from a news reporter.

The traditional way to nominate a cabinet member is to check first with the nominee before announcing the nomination. The right way is also to give the nominee a say in the choice of top subordinates. With no advance notice to Wald, Hillary and Nussbaum had already selected her former law partner, Web Hubbell to be Associate Attorney General, and Philip Heymann to be Deputy A.G. As a result Wald rejected the offer.

Wald had known little about Hubbell other than the facts that he had been Hillary's law partner and Bill Clinton's close friend. But Wald knew a lot about Heymann. She had been an Assistant Attorney General in the Carter Justice Department, when Heymann was a criminal prosecutor—and had launched a "sting" operation that became known as "Abscam."

Heymann had used FBI agents disguised as Arab sheiks to ensnare and indict six Congressmen and one Senator for accepting bribes. All but one of the defendants were pro-labor liberal Democrats who were pledged to support Senator Kennedy's efforts to defeat Carter for re-election in the then upcoming Democratic primaries.

Wald saw Abscam as an unethical political prosecution of Carter's critics. She had let it be known to President Carter that she would resign in protest if Heymann were to proceed to obtain indictments. To silence her Carter promptly "kicked her upstairs"—by nominating her for the Circuit Court of Appeals for the District of Columbia.

Regarding Heymann as unethical and having no say in either his appointment or that of Hubbell, Wald declined the nomination.

After Wald turned down the offer the Clinton'a second choice for Attorney General was Shirley Hufstedler, a former Secretary of Education under President Carter. Like Wald she had also first learned of the offer and the prior appointments of Hubbell and Heymann from the media. Hufstedler also refused the offer.

Hillary's third and fourth choices respectively were her personal friends Zoe Baird and Kimba Wood. Both seemed to be figurehead appointees, but each of them were eventually disqualified for not paying social security taxes for their house maids—scandals known in the media as "Nannygate."

Hillary's fifth choice was Janet Reno, a Florida prosecutor who had been recommended by Hillary's brother Hugh—who lived in Florida and knew Reno well.

In Reno's confirmation hearings before the Senate Judiciary Committee it came out that while prosecutor in Dade County Florida, crime increased 50%. In addition, Republican Senators Hatch and Cohen said that the

Judiciary Committee had received "rumors" of character flaws in the form of excessive drinking and a gender preference for young women. However, Reno was confirmed.

Later an op-ed article about Reno appeared in the Wall Street Journal by Jack Thompson, a Florida lawyer with the highest ratings in ethics by the bar association. Thompson had been opposed to the confirmation—and also appeared on such shows as Nightline, Crossfire and Good Morning America. He described Reno as a "closet" homosexual, who was "subject to bribes and unfit to be Attorney General."

Within Reno's first month the FBI had intentionally fire bombed the Branch Davidian compound at Waco, Texas and killed several innocent people. Athough it later came out that the plans to fire-bomb Waco had been laid before she took office, Reno took the blame. Quoting the famous sign in President Truman's office she stated: "The Buck Stops here."

For the entire eight years of the Clinton presidency Janet Reno was to remain as Attorney General—and incur frequent criticism for her willingness to act as a protective shield for the White House. For example, on October 7, 1997 the New York Times (which had supported Clinton's election and re-election) was to publish an editorial critical of Reno's failure to investigate the Democratic fund raising scandals of 1996, stating: "It has been a full year since Ms. Reno was confronted with initial evidence of the biggest political money scandal in a generation, and her response shows little concern with her place in history as a custodian of the Justice Department . . . Senator Fred Thompson, chairman of the Senate Governmental Affairs Committee, rightly describes Justice as being in 'departmental meltdown.' . . . It would be nice if Senator Thompson's remark could be written off as partisan hyperbole, but the record supports him."

13

Hillary and Health Care

While campaigning for the presidency Bill Clinton repeatedly vowed to reform our health care system. Early in his first term Hillary became head of an official program called the President's Task Force on Health Care Reform—comprised of 600 paid participants from the private sector

Eventually the preparation of her plan was determined by the General Accounting office to cost $13.4 million dollars. In addition it cost the government $434,000.00 for legal fees in defending challenges to the secrecy of its proceedings. Since the task force operated in violation of federal "Sunshine Laws" Hillary and others were fined $285, 864.00. The final plan was 1,324 pages long and was summarily rejected without debate by the Democratic controlled Congress.

Because of Hillary's reputation as a "liberal" a majority of Congressional Democrats had assumed that her final work product would call for a "single payer" system similar to Medicare—and would likewise permit patients to go to doctors of their own choosing. Such a system had also been endorsed by the prestigious *New England Journal of Medicine* and a large number of professional health care organizations.

When the plan was finally unveiled the media called it "Hillarycare"—and had difficulty in explaining its complex details to the public. As Peggy Noonan of the Wall Street Journal later wrote: "Americans would have to choose among unfamiliar new 'purchasing cooperatives' and 'health alliances,' and accept new limits on their choices of doctors and hospitals; 'gatekeepers' would determine who gets to see a specialist, and who the specialist would be. Employers who employed at least a dozen people—would have to pay 80 percent of the premiums for workers and their families."

When the plan was unveiled it was referred to Pat Moynihan the Democratic Senator from New York who was the Chairman of the Senate Committee that had jurisdiction over health care legislation. The author of 18 books and recipient of sixty two honorary degrees, Moynihan was highly respected for his intellectual honesty. After he advised Hillary that he could not support her plan one of her White House aides told *Time* magazine that if Moynihan got in the way "We'll role right over him if we have to."

On the House side liberal Democratic Congressman Pete Stark of San Francisco was Chairman of the Subcommittee on Health of the Ways and Means Committee. He also tried to warn Hillary that her bill was unacceptable. The response to Stark was "Take it or leave it."

In the end neither the Senate Finance Committee nor the House Ways and Means Committee bothered to hold hearings on the bill.

Of all the criticism of the Clinton White House one of the most incisive was by New York *Times* editor Abe Rosenthal—who over his entire career has been a bulwark of support for liberal Democratic causes. He wrote: "In concept, the First Ladyship is an affront to American democracy. In practice it skews the administration of government, evades anti-nepotism statutes and avoids the responsibility that should go with authority. It is the only political post that demands the essential qualification of being married to a particular man at a particular time in his life . . . . Seen and used as a job the First Ladyship has become a government center. In lieu of salary it provides the jobholder with staff, luxury, and that most important of all perks—power."

14

Friends in Office

By the end of the Clinton presidency many of their friends and key aides were forced to resign for ethical violations or to face criminal charges. The first two Clinton appointees forced to resign were their closest advisors on legal matters. One was chief White House counsel Bernard Nussbaum, who had been Hillary's supervisor on the Nixon impeachment staff. The other was Associate Attorney General Webster Hubbell.

Hubbell, whom Clinton often described as his "closest friend," had been Hillary Clinton's partner in the Rose law firm in Arkansas. He stepped down from his position as Associate Attorney General on April 8, 1994 to face criminal charges for defrauding the Rose firm and its clients of some $400,000 by submitting false bills. Eventually he pleaded guilty to two felony counts, and was sentenced to 1 1/2 years in prison.

In July 1993, early in Hubbell's tenure in the Clinton administration he and Nussbaum had forced the FBI's then-Director William Sessions, a former federal judge, to resign. At what the press was to report as a "shoot out" they chastised him for having taken his wife on his government airplane and for claiming a tax deduction for using the trunk of his private car for carrying firearms for law enforcement purposes. They insisted that he resign prior to the expiration of his ten year term—a term established by an act of Congress to insure the political independence of the FBI Director.

According to press reports Hubbell told the FBI director: "Resign or be fired! Today!" On the way out of the meeting Sessions stumbled on the curb and broke his elbow. He resigned shortly thereafter. With Hillary's approval the directorship of the FBI was then entrusted to Judge Louis Freeh of New York, a close friend of Nussbaum.

Under Freeh, on the request of Nussbaum, the FBI was soon unlawfully to provide the White House with more than 900 raw FBI files mostly of Republican leaders and political opponents of President Clinton—creating a scandal described by the media as "Filegate."

Nussbaum also recruited the FBI to participate in a politically inspired plan to purge employees of its travel office and replace them with employees of an Arkansas based travel agency that had helped finance President Clinton's election campaign. The result was a scandal that the media described as "Travelgate."

As questionable as was Nussbaum's role in these matters the scandal that lead to his removal related to the death of Deputy White House counsel Vincent Foster—a former law partner of Hillary Clinton and Webster Hubbell. Following the discovery of Foster's body in a park Nussbaum aggressively impeded the investigation of Foster's death.

On March 4, 1994 an editorial appeared in the New York Times entitled *White House Ethics Meltdown*, stating: "It is, of course, long past time for Mr. Nussbaum to be dismissed. He seems to conceive of his being 'the President's lawyer' as a license to meddle with the integrity of any federal agency. First, he and his staff tried to involve the Federal Bureau of Investigation in a politically inspired White House purge of employees of its travel office. When Vincent Foster, the deputy counsel, committed suicide, Mr. Nussbaum interfered with the investigation by the National Park Service and transferred secret files to Mr. Clinton's private lawyer. All this paints a picture of a White House dedicated to short-cutting justice if that is what it takes to shield the financial affairs of Mr. Clinton and his wife from scrutiny. This president desperately needs first rate legal advice and a staff that is under someone's management control." Following the publication of the editorial President Clinton requested Nussbaum's resignation.

Another close friend of both of the Clintons, and among the first to be appointed to a White House position, was Patsy Thomasson. A long time member of the Clinton's innermost circle of Arkansas friends, Thomasson was appointed as a special assistant to the President and eventually became the White House Director of Administration and Personnel.

Following the death of Vincent Foster, when the police requested that his office be sealed, Thomasson was the first person to ignore the request and begin searching the office.

Of all of President Clinton's appointees Thomasson had close ties to an Arkansas drug scandal and came to Washington with perhaps the most questionable background. Prior to her White House assignment Thomasson had been the chief business assistant of Dan Lasater, an Arkansas bond dealer and multi-millionaire who had previously been one of Clinton's earliest financial backers. He had been a member of Clinton's "kitchen circle" and enjoyed an access to the back door of the Governor's Mansion in Little Rock that was as unlimited as the access of members of Clinton's own family.

In 1986 Lasater had been indicted for "knowingly and intentionally conspiring to possess and to distribute cocaine." In connection with his prosecution it was established that Lasater had loaned Roger Clinton, the governor's then-cocaine addicted half-brother, $8,000.00 to pay a drug related debt. Roger Clinton, who himself was likewise convicted of dealing in cocaine under Lasater's supervision, had been employed by Lasater to work both as a driver and to work on a horse farm connected with cocaine trafficking.

In his trial Lasater admitted to giving free cocaine to his friends, including providing ashtrays full of it on his corporate jet. He had also given Bill and Hillary Clinton free use of the same corporate jet.

After being sentenced to 2 ½ years in an Arkansas prison Lasater had given Patsy Thomasson—who still enjoyed close ties to the Clintons—a power of attorney with authority over all of his financial affairs. After serving only six months in prison Lasater was pardoned by Governor Clinton—who also restored Lasater's revoked license to broker bonds for the state.

One of Patsy Thomasson's principle duties in the Clinton White House was to make sure that the staff had appropriate security clearances and that they abstained from drug use. According to Gary Aldrich, an FBI agent who eventually resigned from the White House staff in protest, Thomasson breached her responsibilities.

The roles of Nussbaum, Hubbell, and Thomasson are but a few examples of the questionable conduct of the many "Friends of Bill and Hill.' At the highest levels of the government four members of the Clinton cabinet were also implicated in major criminal and ethical violations.

President Clinton's first Secretary of Agriculture, Mike Espy—a black former Congressman from Mississipi—was indicted in the District of Columbia on 39 felony charges that include mail and wire fraud, violations of the Meat Inspection Act of 1907, taking illegal gratuities of more than

$35,000, making false statements and tampering with a witness. He was acquitted by an all black jury.

Another cabinet member, Secretary of Commerce Ron Brown, who was killed in a plane crash in Bosnia in April 1996, died within two weeks of being indicted for bribery. Prior to his death Brown had been under investigation by two grand juries, the Senate Judiciary Committee, the Commerce Department's Inspector General, the Justice Department, the FDIC, and the House Government Reform and Oversight Committee.

Another cabinet member to be involved in scandal was former Secretary of Housing and Urban Development Henry Cisneros. His ethical troubles began in July 1994, when a former campaign aide and girlfriend, Linda Medlar, sued Cisneros claiming that he reneged on a promise to pay her $4,000-a-month after they ended a much-publicized affair. In his background interview Cisneros originally told the FBI that he had paid Medlar no more than $10,000 to $15,000. However, Medlar's financial records later revealed that the total payments were $213,000.

Still another Clinton Cabinet member to resign under a criminal cloud was Secretary of Energy Hazel O'Leary, who was charged by Congressional investigators with excessive foreign travel. In June 1996 the Energy Department's Inspector General issued a 183-page report confirming that sixteen of her foreign trips cost taxpayers more than $4.5 million and in spending money that was not legally authorized.

In addition to cabinet members, other high level Clinton appointees were also the subject of criminal proceedings. More than 30 officials of the Clinton administration were investigated, indicted, convicted or forced to resign.

Three associates of Hillary and Bill Clinton pleaded the 5th amendment privilege against self incrimination—and at least three others fled the country. In addition, more than 100 persons involved in raising money for the Clintons' 1996 campaign also took the 5th amendment.

15

Whitewater

The questionable real estate transactions that came to be known as "Whitewater" began one night in August of 1978 at a dinner meeting that Hillary and Bill Clinton had with James and Susan McDougal. At that time James McDougal, then thirty-eight, was a well known figure in Arkansas politics. In 1961, at age 19 he had run John Kennedy's successful campaign in the state. McDougal then went to Washington to work for Arkansas Senator John McClellan, and later for Senator William Fulbright.

McDougal and the Bill Clinton had first met in 1968, when McDougal had managed Senator Fulbright's re-election campaign. McDougal was later helpful in getting Clinton, then a college student, a part-time job in Senator Fulbright's office. From the beginning of Clinton's political career in Arkansas McDougal had been a personal mentor and financial supporter. By the time of their dinner meeting in 1978 Clinton was considered an odds-on favorite to be elected Governor of Arkansas. While dining at the Black-Eyed Pea Restaurant in Little Rock, James and Susan McDougal offered the Clintons a partnership interest in a land development project—an offer that they apparently could not refuse.

For a price of more than $200,000 the corporation would purchase 230 riverfront acres where Arkansas' popular White River crossed Crooked Creek. In effect, the purchase was with no down payment. Some $183,000 was loaned by a bank run by one of the sellers. The balance of $20,000 was loaned without security by Union National, a Little Rock bank whose board included one of Clinton's main political fund raisers.

James and Susan McDougal guaranteed repayment to the banks of almost $200,000 of the total loans. The McDougals also managed the business and assumed the risks. The Clintons were given a 50% ownership at no cost—even though they provided no capital or collateral and thus had no financial risk. They also claimed immediate tax benefits. For interest paid on the loan by the partnership they deducted $10,000 in 1978 and $12,000 in 1979.

After Bill Clinton's election as governor Hillary was promoted to a partnership in the Rose firm. McDougal's bank became her client at a retainer of $2,000 per month. Governor Clinton appointed McDougal to his official staff giving him oversight over the Department of Economic Development, the Securities and Bank Commission, and the Department of Highway and Transportation.

For the next decade Hillary and the McDougals orchestrated a convoluted series of violations of banking laws and income tax laws.

When Bill Clinton first ran for president Whitewater became a national political issue. On March 8, 1992 during the Democratic primary campaign, reporter Jeff Gerth of the New York Times revealed that Hillary and Bill had received improper loans and filed false income tax returns—claiming deductions for interest that they had not paid. During the same period, referring to Bill Clinton as the "scandal-a-week candidate," former California governor Jerry Brown made similar Whitewater-related charges.

With other candidates and the press looking for scandals Vincent Foster and Webster Hubbell (who were then Hillary's law partners) secretly removed the firm's only copies of files relating to Madison Guaranty as well other Rose clients for whom Hillary had performed legal services. The files, which were legally the property of the clients, were removed without the firm's consent and were later stored in Hubbell's Washington home after he was appointed Associate Attorney General. In addition, Hubbell and Foster were able to obtain computer print-outs of the Rose firm's billing records relating to Hillary Clinton's representation of Madison Guaranty. The records were later subpoenaed by Independent Counsel Robert Fiske in early 1994—and later by the Senate Whitewater Committee in October 1995. But they were no longer to be found.

Also Hillary's billing records that "disappeared" were those relating to another questionable land deal and loan exchange scheme of McDougal's known as Castle Grande. The project benefited Webster Hubbell's father in law, Seth Ward. In 1988 bank regulators had charged that Castle Grande was a "sham" that cost federal taxpayers $4 million.

In 1992 and 1993 Hillary Clinton had denied that she had done any legal work for McDougal or Madison. In April 1994 it was learned that some of the Rose law firms Whitewater-related documents had been shredded. When asked by reporters what she knew about the shredding Hillary said: "Nothing! Absolutely not! It didn't happen, and I know nothing about any other such stories."

In May 1995, Hillary provided federal investigators written responses under oath. She denied any knowledge of Castel Grande—and stating that she had "no recollection" of doing legal work for Seth Ward.

In January 1996 Hillary admitted in written answers to federal banking officials that in 1988—the year in which regulators first began investigating Castle Grand—she had ordered the shredding of 3 Castle Grande files. As for the Whitewater files she eventually stated through her attorney that she "may have" reviewed them during the 1992 campaign but denied any knowledge of their whereabouts. Hubbell was later to testify that he last saw the records during the 1992 presidential campaign in the possession of Vincent Foster.

On July 17, 1993 Foster was found dead in Washington's Fort Marcy Park and had apparently committed suicide.

Following the discovery of Foster's body White House Counsel Bernard Nussbaum initially promised Deputy Attorney General Philip Heymann and Justice Department investigators full access to the files in Foster's office. However, Hillary insisted that investigators be denied "unfettered access" to Foster's files. Nussbaum then reversed himself, reneged on his promise to the Justice Department, and began to obstruct the investigation.

Requests by the Justice Department and park police to seal-off Foster's office were ignored—giving an opportunity to White House aides to remove some of Foster's files. Nussbaum also asserted that he alone would first examine Foster's files and decide which documents to make available to Justice Department investigators. He also asserted that as White House Counsel he would be present at interrogations of witnesses by the FBI and the police.

Congressional investigators learned that after Nussbaum had initially searched Foster's brief case he had declared it empty. Later, one of Nussbaum's aides purportedly searched the brief case and found torn-up pieces of a note by Foster expressing bitterness about his life in Washington. When Nussbaum met with investigators and produced an envelope containing the pieces of the note, the pieces fell out of the envelope on to the floor.

Nussbaum soon clashed with Deputy Attorney General Heymann, who later quietly resigned to return to a teaching position at the Harvard Law

School. Later, in sworn testimony to the Senate Whitewater Committee Heymman said that he had objected to Nussbaum's conduct and asked him, "Bernie are you hiding something?" Heymann also testified that because of the obstruction of the investigation he warned the Clinton White House of a "major disaster brewing."

As congressional investigators continued to probe events related to Foster's death they learned that he had been engaged in preparing responses to expected Whitewater questions. He was also given the responsibility for the preparation of the Clintons' tax returns for 1992 to reflect properly the sale of their shares in Whitewater.

Nussbaum was not alone in searching Foster's unsealed office on the night of his death. Others included President Clinton's aide Patsy Thomasson, and Margaret Williams, Hillary's Chief of Staff. Although each denied under oath that they had removed any documents, Ms. Williams testimony was contradicted by a Secret Service agent who testified that he saw her leave Foster's office on the night of his death with a stack of thick file folders.

Five days after Foster's death Nussbaum, without preparing an inventory, turned over a number of files to Ms. Williams who transferred them to the White House residence. In the ensuing efforts to obtain the missing files a number of subpoenas were issued by congressional committees and independent counsel, Kenneth Starr.

Under subpoena to produce her records relating to Whitewater and the Madison Bank, Hillary stated through her personal counsel that she "may have" seen them during the 1992 campaign but did not know their present whereabouts.

Eventually, a house keeper at the Clinton's private living quarters in the White House found the records by accident in the First Family's private library. Hillary denied any knowledge of how they got there.

16

Webster Hubbell

In 1994, then-Whitewater Independent Counsel Robert Fiske discovered that Hubbell, had over-billed his clients at the Rose law firm $482,410 and that he owed $143,437 in unpaid income taxes. He was then indicted and resigned his high position in the Clinton Justice Department, He pleaded guilty and eventually went to prison.

Ironically Hubbell was to receive much more money by far from being prosecuted than he would have earned had he stayed in the Justice Department. As was first reported on NBC's Nightly News the Clintons arranged for the payment to Hubbell of "hush money" to obtain his silence on their roles in the Whitewater scandal.

Initially it was reported that in the months between his resignation and his incarceration Hubbell received payments of $400,000. Later, House investigators found that Hubbell received $1 million or more, of which $300,000 came from the Riady family of Indonesia, who had been close friends and financial backers of the Clinton since early in their Arkansas days.

In response to questions by the media and congressional investigators the Clinton's initially denied any knowledge of payments to Hubbell. They later changed their explanation, stating that at the time the payments were made to Hubbell the White House did not know that Hubbell was facing a jail sentence.

By May 5, 1997, the evidence of the Clintons' guilt in arranging for the bribery of Hubbell was so compelling that New York Times editor A.M. Rosenthal wrote: "It is impossible for me to believe it happened the way

President Clinton and his wife said it had. I [have] rejected, for myself, the story that neither they nor anybody else at the White House knew that when their good friend Webster L. Hubbell resigned as Associate Attorney General in 1994 he was facing the likelihood of criminal accusations that could land him in jail. They did . . . It would not take a particularly suspicious mind—let alone a prosecutor's—to see high-paying jobs as hush money to keep a defendant silent."

For those of us who had known and worked with Hillary on the Nixon impeachment her role in the obstruction of the investigations of Whitewater now has a sad irony. She and Nussbaum obviously knew that the role of Nixon's White House counsel, John Dean, in the cover-up of Watergate was a basis for charging Nixon with an impeachable offense. In 1972 following the arrest of Watergate burglar Howard Hunt and others. John Dean alone had personally examined the contents of Hunt's White House safe and ordered that they be burned. On behalf of Nixon he had also participated in the payment of hush money to Watergate burglar Howard Hunt.

For his acts Dean had been charged with obstructing justice and served a prison term. In the case of Nixon an article of impeachment by the House Judiciary Committee had charged him with *Approving, condoning, and acquiescing in the surreptitious payment of substantial sums of money for the purpose of obtaining the silence or influencing the testimony of witnesses.*

17

An Indonesian Monopoly

The payments to Webster Hubbell, and other financial support for the Clinton's by the Riady's over many years culminated in granting the Riady enterprises in Indonesia a monopoly on what environmentalists call "clean burning coal."

Such coal has sufficiently low sulfur content to meet strict environmental standards. The Indonesian deposits of environmentally safe coal are the second largest in the world. The world's largest deposits of such coal include 62 billion tons—and are in the United States in southern Utah. However, our deposits can no longer be mined.

On September 18, 1996 Bill Clinton signed an executive order converting 1.7 million acres that contain the coal into a park area the size of Connecticut. By presidential order it became "The Grand Staircase Escalante National Monument" and coal mining was prohibited.

A few weeks after the signing of the executive order, a person inexplicably identified as an unemployed gardener gave the Clinton campaign $400,000. It was eventually revealed that it had come from Arief Wiriadinata and his wife Soraya, whose father was an executive of a Riady owned conglomerate.

At a televised press conference in Utah six weeks before his re=election Bill Clinton proclaimed the need to preserve the natural beauty of the remote area, describing it as a "beautiful, exotic place." At that time the only published report suggesting other concerns appeared in an obscure mining newsletter, in which an unknown reporter, Susan Foster, wrote: "With a stroke of his pen President Clinton wiped out the only significant competition to Indonesian coal interests in the world market."

The President's decision to issue the order was made without prior consultation with Utah Governor Michael Leavitt or any members of Utah's congressional delegation. It stunned Utah's lone congressional Democrat, Bill Orton, in whose district the clean-burning coal is found. It also came as a shock to Louise Liston, the commissioner from Escalante County, who said: "President Clinton has locked up a treasure house that could be used for our children and to boost our economy. We don't know why he would want to do that. Why would he put our nation at risk?"

Subsequently the answer was found in the records of the Federal Elections Commission. Before signing the executive order the Clinton campaign had illegally received a total of more than $1.5 million from the Riady enterprises.

These were not the only illegal campaign contributions to the Clintons from foreign sources.

18

The China Connection

In the 1992 campaign against President George H. W. Bush the Clintons had charged the Bush administration with granting China "favored nation" trading status and fostering a $19 billion annual trade deficit at the expense of American workers. Criticizing President Bush for being insensitive to the Tiananmen Square killings of students in 1989, the Clinton campaign charged the Bush administration with sacrificing the human rights of Chinese workers and students in favor of trade with an oppressive communist regime.

Clinton pledged that if elected he would end China's "favored-nation" status and reduce the unfavorable balance of trade in which annual Chinese imports into the United States exceeded our exports to China by $19 billion.

In March 1993, less than two months after President Clinton's inauguration Mochtar Riady, patriarch of the Lippo conglomerate, wrote a personal letter to Clinton—urging him, in effect, to ignore his campaign promises. Riady urged the new administration to pursue a vigorous policy of economic engagement with China. Early in his first term President Clinton reversed his policy and implemented Riady's recommendation.

Beginning in 1993 President Clinton pursued policies that were described as a "Vision for Asia" that were implemented by Secretary of Commerce Ron Brown, and former Lippo executive John Huang as Deputy Assistant Secretary. The policies granted most-favored-nation status to China and intensified economic engagement. By the time President Clinton was to run for re-election in 1996 the annual trade deficit with China was to more than double, to $40 billion.

In an article in the New York Times by Robert E. Lighthizer, a deputy U.S. Trade Representative in the Reagan administration, addressed the question of campaign contributions relating to China, stating: "Certainly the money was not directed at insuring that most-favored-nation trade status continues to be extended to China. Mr. Clinton tossed in the towel on that issue a long time ago. Much more likely, the money was meant to influence the decision on whether China should be permitted to join the World Trade Organization and, if so, on what terms. This is far and away the most important trade issue between the two countries."

On July 8, 1997 Senator Fred Thompson, chairman of the Senate Committee on Governmental Affairs, opened hearings on the financing of the 1996 election campaigns with the following statement: "I would like to turn our attention to one of the most troublesome areas of this investigation. I speak of allegations concerning a plan hatched during the last election cycle by the Chinese government and designed to pour illegal money into American political campaigns. The plan had a goal: to buy access and influence and furtherance of Chinese government interests . . . The committee believes that high-level Chinese government officials crafted the plan to increase China's influence over the U.S. political process."

According to a profile compiled from Washington Post and washingtonpost.com staff reports: "At the heart of the Senate investigation into fund-raising improprieties sits John Huang While a mid-level Commerce Department official, Huang enjoyed extraordinary access to President Clinton. He also attended dozens of briefings involving classified information, even as he maintained ties to the Lippo Group the Indonesian conglomerate for which he had been head of U.S. operations."

The Clintons had first befriended Huang in Arkansas in 1980 when he and the Riadys first began to help finance their political campaigns. In 1993 five months before he began serving under Ron Brown in the Commerce Department—and while still an employee of Lippo Enterprises—Huang received a top-secret security clearance, with access to classified CIA and FBI information.

In granting the clearance the normal background investigation of candidates for such a clearance was waived by the Commerce Department's Chief of Personnel Security, Paul Buskirk, who wrote in a memorandum: "Huang is granted this waiver due to the critical need for his expertise in the new administration for Secretary Brown." It was also learned that during his entire tenure as a government official Huang never underwent an overseas background check despite his employment in Hong Kong by Lippo in 1984 and 1985.

When Huang resigned from the Commerce Department to become finance vice chairman of the Democratic National Committee he in effect took his official security clearance with him. Even though he was a political fund-raiser Huang was issued a "consultant top-secret" clearance on December 12, 1995. Although he was in fact never employed as a government consultant the clearance remained in effect until after the 1996 presidential campaign.

In the summer of 1996 Huang's success at raising campaign money was cited by the President, who at a Democratic fundraiser said: "And I'd like to thank my long-time friend, John Huang, for being so effective." Later a Commerce Department official was quoted by the Wall Street Journal and the Los Angeles Times: "Mr. John Huang was in a perfect position to influence U.S foreign policy. He had all the information, he had access to CIA information. He was in a position to influence the State Department."

During the 1996 campaign Huang was a frequent visitor at the White House and pressed the Clintons on matters related to Indonesia, China, and Asia in general. Among other questionable activities some of Huang's records show that he attended policy meetings with Chinese government officials at China's Washington embassy.

Most of the records of Huang's activities at the Democratic National Committee were not made available to Congress despite requests for them. Reported as missing were details of his visits to the White House, telephone logs, outgoing correspondence and travel records—as well as records of business that he conducted from places other than his office at the Democratic National Committee.

In January 1997 Assistant Secretary of Commerce Kramer disclosed that Huang had been given at least 37 intelligence briefings. In addition, Huang had access to 15 classified field reports and at least 12 intelligence documents, and received classified materials on nine other occasions.

Records obtained by Congress later showed that after receiving classified documents on at least two occasions Huang promptly made three telephone calls to the Lippo Bank in Los Angeles. On one of those occasions, he also scheduled a meeting with Chinese officials. Huang's phone logs show a total of 70 calls to the Lippo Bank, as well as other calls to Arkansas businessmen and lawyers with financial ties to Asia. Huang also visited the Chinese embassy at least six times while he was at the Commerce department.

In addition, Huang also had an office arrangement with Stephens Inc., an Arkansas investment banking company with close ties to Lippo as well as to President and Mrs. Clinton that date back to the 1980s. Huang frequently used the Stephen company's Washington office as often as two or three times per week to make telephone calls and to send faxes while at the Commerce Department.

On June 30, 1997, it was announced that Congress was able to acquire even more evidence about Huang. As was reported in the Washington Times:

"The chairman of a House committee said yesterday that secret intelligence briefings John Huang received while serving as a top Commerce Department official included information that could have resulted in the death of a CIA informant.

"Rep. Gerald B.H. Solomon, New York Republican and chairman of the House Rules Committee, described the briefings as 'extremely serious and dangerous' and asked President Clinton to make White House officials who knew about them available to congressional investigators . . .

"Mr. Solomon has said electronic intercepts show Mr. Huang 'committed economic espionage and breached our national security' by passing classified data to Lippo."

Despite the large quantity of documented evidence of Huang's violation of criminal laws designed to protect national security on August 12, 1999 Attorney General Janet Reno approved a plea bargain with Huang charging him only with violating campaign finance laws and sentencing him to one year of probation, a fine, and community service. (Ironically, Huang's community service was to "educate Asian Americans about how to get into U.S. politics.")

19

Other Foreign Policies

During his 1992 campaign against President G.H.W. Bush Bill Clinton had pledged to retain a then 30-year old trade embargo on Vietnam unless we obtained a "full accounting" of Americans missing in action during the Vietnam War. However, according to charges later made to the Justice Department Commerce Secretary-designate Ron Brown accepted $700,000 from a Vietnamese businessman to help lift the Trade Embargo.

Several months after President Clinton's inauguration in 1993 Mochtar Riady led a trade mission of Asian bankers to Vietnam to appraise business opportunities there. During the same period Riady's Lippo Group was seeking White House and Commerce Department help in expanding its $6.9 billion real estate and investment holdings into Vietnam. Later, despite a determination by the State Department that Vietnam was still holding missing Americans President Clinton decided to lift the embargo on Vietnam.

Another questionable foreign policy decision related to immigration laws. On February 11, 1996 President Clinton reiterated his support for lowering the level of legal immigration as recommended by the Commission on Immigration Reform. Consistent with the Commission's recommendation the President opposed granting a so called "sibling preference"—which would allow foreign born brothers and sisters of naturalized Americans to immigrate to the United States.

John Huang, who by then had resigned from the Commerce Department and become a fund-raiser, was a strong supporter of sibling preference. In preparation for a February 17, 1996 fund raiser for Asian Americans, Huang wrote a memo to the President describing sibling preference as a top priority among Asian American voters. At a dinner with the President at the Hay-Adams Hotel, $1 million dollars was raised—with 40 Asian American couples each contributing $25,000. On March 20, a month after raising $1 million dollars from advocates of sibling preference President Clinton reversed himself and informed Congress that he favored granting citizenship to brothers and sisters of naturalized Americans. In September 1996 he signed a bill granting the preference. Still another foreign policy decision subject to campaign contributions was influenced by Mark Jimenez, a Miami computer executive whose company, Future Tech Internatonal, sold computer parts in Latin America, including Paraguay.

In a letter to Attorney General Janet Reno signed by House Judiciary Committee Chairman Henry Hyde and 19 other members of the committee wrote:

"Since 1993 Mr. Jimenez and his employees have given over $800,000 to the Democratic Party, the Clinton—Gore campaign, and other initiatives linked to President Clinton. Jimenez has visited the White House at least 12 times since April 1994, and on at least seven of these occasions, he met personally with President Clinton.

"The timing of some of these donations strongly suggests that there was a quid pro quo. From February through April 1996, Mr. Jimenez and various officials of the government of Paraguay met in the White House with presidential adviser and former chief of staff, Mack McClarty, regarding threats to the government of Paraguay. On March 1, the State Department recommended that Paraguay no longer receive American foreign aid because it had not done anything to stop drug smugglings. President Clinton then issued a waiver allowing the continued aid despite the State Department's finding.

"On April 22, the military of Paraguay attempted a coup against the President of Paraguay, Carlos Wasmosy. The White House allowed President Wasmosy to take refuge in the American embassy in Asuncion and took other steps to support him. The same day, Mr. Jimenez gave $100,000 to the Democratic National Committee.

"In addition, during February 1996, Mr. Jimenez attended one of the now famous White House coffees. Ten days later he gave another $50,000 to the Democratic National Committee. On September 30, 1996, Mr. Jimenez arranged for a White House tour for a number of business friends who were attending a meeting of the International Monetary Fund. The same day, he sent $75,000 to the Democratic National Committee. The close coincidence of Mr. Jimenez's contributions with the favors he received is highly suspicious.

"The President's direct involvement includes his calling President Wasmoy and his direct participation in the coffee meeting in question. If there was a quid pro quo involved, these incidents may violate 18 U.S.C 201 and other bribery statutes."

Finally, there is also evidence that the President's policies relating to one of our possessions in the Pacific have likewise been improperly influence by campaign contributions. Relying on news sources considered credible the same letter from Judiciary Committee Chairman Hyde also cited still another example of possible bribery charges relating to campaign contributions from Guam. As described in the Hyde letter the evidence is as follows:

"In February, the Washington Post reported that on September 4, 1995, First Lady Hillary Clinton stopped over in Guam on the way to the International Women's Conference in Beijing, China. She ended her visit with a shrimp cocktail buffet hosted by Guam's governor, Carl T. Gutierrez, a Democrat. Three weeks later, a Guam Democratic Party official arrived in Washington with more than $250,000 in campaign contributions. Within six additional months, Governor Gutierrez and a small group of Guam businessmen had produced an additional $132,000 for the Clinton-Gore reelection campaign and $510,000 in soft money for the Democratic National Committee.

"In December 1996, the Administration circulated a memo that would have granted a long sought reversal of the Administration's position on labor and immigration issues in a way that was very favorable to businesses in Guam.

"Some officials attribute the administration's support for the reversal to the money raised for the president's reelection campaign. One senior U.S. official said 'the political side' of her agency had informed her that the administration's shift was linked to campaign contributions. 'We had always opposed giving Guam authority over its own immigration,' the official said. 'But when that $600,000 was paid, the political side switched.' U.S. officials from three other agencies added that they too had been told that the policy shift was linked to money."

Attorney General Reno took no steps to have an independent prosecutor investigate these matters.

20

"Citizenship USA"

In 1995 first lady Hillary Clinton saw an opportunity to win votes in the upcoming presidential elections by accelerating the naturalization of immigrants ready to vote Democratic. As a result she initiated a program known as "Citizens USA" to be headed by Vice President Al Gore. Its goal was to provide citizenship to one million aliens by election day 1996.

In March 1996 Elaine Kamarck, a senior White House adviser appointed by Hillary sent an e-mail message to Gore aide, Doug Farbrother, complaining that the program was not being implelemented fast enough and that "only if the INS processed citizenship applicants seven days a week for up to 12 hours a day can we hope to make a significant enough dent in the backlog that it will show up when it matters." The final result was large numbers of immigrants were naturalized with no effort to ascertain if they had criminal records.

In 1997 Doris M. Meissner, whom President Clinton had appointed to be commissioner of immigration and naturalization, was questioned by Congressman Lamar Smith (R-Texas), the chairman of the House Judiciary's Subcommittee on Immigration. She admitted that in most cases citizenship had been granted without the receipt of a fingerprint report from the FBI. She also acknowledged that she never told the FBI—from which INS was required to request fingerprint checks of aliens applying for citizenship bureau—to anticipate the unprecedented increase to 1.1 million in the number of aliens made citizens in 1996.

Mrs. Meissner further acknowledged that she and INS had ignored a warning given by congressional auditors who had recommended two years earlier that laws be enforced that were intended to prevent criminals from becoming American citizens.

At the time of the first congressional hearings, Attorney General Janet Reno—who had overall supervisory authority over Mrs. Meissner and INS—admitted that the Clinton administration "may have" awarded citizenship to at least 168 aliens convicted of felonies that should have disqualified them. In response to congressional concerns that the number was understated she also directed that INS conduct an internal audit.

On May 23, in response to criticisms of Reno's figure of 168 the INS provided Congress with the results of a still uncompleted audit that found that of the nearly 1.1 million people who were granted citizenship between September 1995 and September 1996 16,400 of the new citizens had a record of at least one felony arrest. It also found 4,946 cases in which a criminal arrest should have disqualified an applicant or in which an applicant lied about this or her criminal history.

Mrs. Meissner also promised to commence denaturalization proceedings against the applicants found to have been disqualified. However only a token number of disqualification cases, if any, were processed.

21

White House for Sale

In 1992 the Clinton campaign had promised to "break the stranglehold the special interests have on our elections and the lobbyists have on our government." Once in the White House they began early in their first term to implement a re-election plan that would raise more money from special interest groups and $100,000 donors than any Democrat in history.

Four years later the Washington Post's famed Watergate reporter Robert Woodward was to note: "The normal shields that even the Nixon White House had in place to check on foreign donors were gone . . . President Clinton figuratively put up a sign on the White House reading, "Bring the money!" Also, as noted in a New York Times editorial in 1997: "What this White House seems to have invented was top-to-bottom integration of government and campaign functions under tight White House control."

In preparation for the campaign, and with Hillary's written endorsement, Bill Clinton had ordered the White House staff to prepare a computerized data base—ostensibly for the purpose of storing the names and information concerning persons to be invited to such official functions as State dinners or be sent mail such as White House Christmas cards. In reality it was used illegally to raise campaign contributions.

As Woodward noted, unlike Nixon the Clintons' solicitations not only included American donors but foreigners as well—even though donations from foreigners were expressly outlawed.

The data base as well as the facilities of the Democratic National Committee were illegally used to offer prospective donors meals and overnight stays in the Lincoln bedroom and other residential rooms in the "family" section of White

House that was traditionally controlled by the First Lady. Other donors were also invited to coffee and teas, a wide variety of ceremonial occasions, and such events as the President's weekly radio address. Still others were invited to take trips on Air Force I and II as well international as missions.

The largest of the Lincoln bedroom donors to the President's campaign included Dirk Ziff, a financier who gave $411,000; movie producer Steven Spielberg, $336,000; retired businessman William Rollnick, $235,000; and Hollywood magnate Lew Wasserman, $225,000. A number of others gave more than $100,000 each before or after sleeping in the Lincoln bed.

White House staff members were so pleased by the fundraising success that they humorously referred to the White House as "Motel 1600."

In addition to the Lincoln bedroom the President also held 103 coffee meetings with some 1300 other large donors in the White House Map Room—with the DNC raising almost $27 million in connection with such events.

Along with laws prohibiting campaign contributions from foreign sources a variety of other laws violated by the President, the First Lady, and their aides fell into several categories. One set of laws prohibits the use of government facilities and of the working time of federal employees to raise campaign contributions. Other laws were enacted in 1974 as an outgrowth of Watergate and make limits on campaign it illegal for an individual to contribute more than $1,000 to a Federal candidate per election or more than $20,000 per year to a political party for candidate election expenses. These strictly limited contributions are known as "hard money" and are used for direct candidate support.

The election laws also draw a distinction between "hard money" contributions to the campaigns of political candidates and "soft" money" which cannot be used to promote individual candidates—and can be used only in issue-oriented activities that are not tied to an election campaign The raising of "soft" money is not subject to dollar limitations on individual or corporate contributions.

In the Clinton presidency the distinctions between "soft" money and "hard" money became blurred. As a candidate the President personally not only solicited "soft" money but also directed its use during his campaign. As President Clinton's campaign strategist Dick Morris has noted in his book, *Behind the Oval Office*: "The President became the day-to-day operational director of our TV-ad campaign. He worked every script, watched each ad, ordered changes in every visual presentation, and decided which ads would run and where . . . Every line of every ad came under *his* critical, and often meddlesome gaze."

In violation of the election laws the Democratic National Committee transferred at least $2 million in "soft" money contributions into "hard" accounts and spent it directly on the re-election campaign of President Clinton and other candidates. Federal Election Commission records and interviews with Democratic contributors show that the money transfers often were made without the permission or knowledge of the contributors, causing at least 62 donors to give more than the lawful annual maximum of $25,000 in contributions to all federal campaigns.

In addition, the Democratic National Committee also transferred some $32 million in "soft" money accounts to various state Democratic parties. This was done as part of an elaborate scheme to by-pass the limits imposed by the election laws on the amounts that the campaign could legally spend on advertising—limits that the Clinton-Gore campaign had agreed to accept in return for receiving public funds.

Hillary Clinton, her White House staff and office in particular were used to solicit and receive campaign money illegally. Her office was frequently visited by Johnny Chung, a Chinese-American entrepreneur who had known the Clintons in Arkansas. Chung made a total of $366,000 in contributions to the 1996 campaign—which when exposed after the election as illegal were eventually refunded.

Of 50 visits to the White House Chung was cleared to enter 21 times by Hillary Clinton's office. Subsequently, Chung took the 5th Amendment to avoid testifying before congressional committees In an interview by the Los Angeles times reported on July 27, 1997 Chung stated, "I see the White House is like a subway—you have to put in coins to open the gates."

Congressional investigators also learned that through Hillary's office Chung brought six businessmen donors from China into the White House where they had their picture taken with Mrs. Clinton, had lunch in the White House, and watched the President deliver his weekly radio address.

During many of his more than 50 visits to the White House Chung brought other business leaders from China and other Asian countries—from whom it was illegal to receive contributions either directly or indirectly. On at least one occasion DNC finance director Richard Sullivan objected to such visits, but was over-ruled by the White House.

On August 22, 1997 in an editorial entitled *The White House Turn Stile* the New York Times commented on still other activities that Chung had disclosed to Tom Brokaw of NBC News:

"Mr. Chung said he gave $50,000 to a White House aide to help pay for a Christmas reception in the executive mansion, and then landed a meeting with the First Lady. Hillary Rodham Clinton said she had no recollection of such a meeting, and the White House denies that it solicited the money from Mr. Chung. But the NBC News report was filled with pictures of Mr. Chung lounging around the executive mansion like a guest at a resort hotel. There he was in the White House mess hall, or at the President's movie theater, or at the White House bowling alley . . . There can be no cleaning up of the record of the Clinton campaign's reckless fund-raising for the 1996 campaign."

22

Leaving the White House

Throughout most of the Clinton presidency Democratic leaders and journalists had generally remained silent regarding the misdeeds of Bill and Hillary Clinton. But in their last week in the White House the Clinton offended the sensibilities of some fellow Democrats who finally speak out.

Before departing the Clintons took moving vans filled with government property from the White House, including china, antiques, and other furnishings. They solicited hundreds of thousands of dollars worth of lavish gifts to furnish their new homes and offices. More than 140 last minute pardons were granted that were highly questionable.

Al Hunt of the Wall Street Journal and previously Bill Clinton's staunchest defender on NBC's *Capital Gang* said on February 24, 2001: "They leave a stain that is bigger than anything in impeachment . . . I think the damage is severe. I think it is lasting. It's on Bill Clinton's legacy. It's on Hillary Clinton, and it may well be on the Democratic Party."

Jimmy Breslin, New York's colorful liberal Democratic columnist, had first met Hillary when she worked on the Nixon impeachment. He had never before criticized her publicly. On January 31, 2001 he wrote (in normally pro-Clinton *Newsday*) : "Bill Clinton was taking arm chairs and coffee tables as he left the White House . . . Every time Hillary Clinton passes a bank the alarm goes off. Her name now and forever more is Senator Shoplift."

Maureen Dowd of the New York Times wrote that the Clintons "tore up the joint in the wee hours and then left the scene." Paul Goldman of the Democratic National Committee published an article in the Wall Street Journal of February 15, 2001 titled *Democrats Must Censure Clinton,* stating

"Clinton didn't just take the White House China, he took its soul and flushed it down the toilet."

The eleventh hour pardons generated even more criticism from Democrats who had previously remained silent through out the Clinton presidency. They were granted contrary to strict guidelines that had been in place in the office of the Justice Departments pardon attorneys and followed by past administrations.

One of the last minute pardons particularly involved Hillary. A group of Hasidic Jews had set up a community known as New Square in Rockland County, New York. In 1999 six of their leaders had been convicted in Brooklyn for a scam involving the swindling of $40 million in federal funds in the form of fictitious Pell Grants.

Hillary had visited New Square in her campaign for the Senate and promised to help, New Square residents voted for her 1,400 to 12. They were pardoned by Bill Clinton on his last day in office in disregard of Justice Department guidelines.

Two other pardons were granted to Edward and Jo Gregory over the strenuous objections of the Justice Department. They had been convicted of bank fraud in 1982. The pardons came in March 2000 during Hillary's hotly contested Senate Campaign—to which the Gregory's made contributions.

The guidelines were also ignored to grant pardons to several felons who had paid Hillary's brother Hugh Rodham fees of $4,000 for representing them.

The most notorious pardon of all was of Marc Rich, a multi-national financier who was on the FBI's most wanted list. Rich had ties to Castro in Cuba and Gaddafi in Libya, had abandoned his American citizen, and fled to Switzerland to escape arrest here.

Rich and his wife then had an extraordinarily amicable divorce and she began to represent him in the United States. In her late fifties she was ebullient, flamboyant, and full figured. She was frequently a welcomed visitor at the White House. Prior to the pardon she had helped to arrange large numbers of fund raisers for the Clintons with her wealthy friends. She gave two chairs and two coffee tables to the Clintons worth $7,375 and an expensive Saxophone to Bill. She had also been one of the first big donors to the Clinton library.

The Rich pardon was too much for some of the Clinton's most ardent prior Democratic supporters to attempt to condone. Democratic Senator Joe Biden of Delaware said "I think the President had an incredible lapse of memory or was brain dead." Liberal Massachusetts Congressman Barney Frank said: "It was a terrible thing he did . . . It was just abusive. These are people who forgot where the line was between public service and what was personally convenient for them."

One of the most comprehensive criticisms of the Clintons was by President Carter's former Chief of Staff, Hamilton Jordan. Crippled since 1985 by three bouts of cancer since1985 he no longer had any professional ties to the Democratic party which might have restrained him from speaking his mind about the Clintons. On February 21, 2001 Jordon published an article in the Wall Street Journal titled *The First Grifters,* stating:

"When one considers pardons for political friends and donors, gifts to the White House taken by the Clintons for their personal use, and the attempt to lease extravagant penthouse offices for the former president with taxpayer money, a word comes to mind: grifters—a term used in the Great Depression to describe fast-talking con artists who roamed the countryside, profiting at the expense of the poor and the uneducated, always one step ahead of the law, moving on before they were held accountable for their schemes and half-truths.

"No longer able to dominate the national news with moving speeches or policy initiatives, the First Grifters have been unable to move beyond the Marc Rich pardon, White House gifts and other events related to their noisy and ungraceful departure from office. Robbed of the frills of high office, we can now examine these last-minute pardons—and the Clintons—for what they are.

"It is difficult for the average citizen to comprehend how outrageous Bill Clinton's pardons are to those of us who have worked in the White House. While the president's right to grant a pardon is unequivocal, certain procedures have evolved over time that are honored and passed along from president to president. These include: a formal, written analysis of the case by the Justice Department; a description of the crime and a history of the trial; recommendations of the prosecuting team that won the conviction; a listing of the substantive argument for and against the pardon and a statement of any extenuating circumstances that justify the review of the case.

"Yet there was no effort to formally collect opinions from the key parties in the Marc Rich case. Indeed, the 11th-hour presentation of the request to Mr. Clinton was made by Mr. Rich's attorney, Jack Quinn, who happens to be a former Clinton White House counsel . . . We do know that Mr. Clinton found time to confer with his political advisers, party fundraisers, Denise Rich, and her friends."

Jordan's article also raised the psychological question of how such astute politicians as the Clintons could have believed they could have gotten away with the transgressions of their last days in the White House. His theory is: "If a president can get caught having sex in the Oval Office with an intern, and committing perjury about it to a federal grand jury, and still get away with it, what could possibly stop him? Bill Clinton—whose every decision was guided by public opinion polls—interpreted his high job-approval ratings following his impeachment at least as a vote of confidence and more likely as some form of national forgiveness."

In conclusion, the history of Hillary and Bill Clinton is reminiscent of philosopher George Santayana's admonition: "Those who cannot remember the past are condemned to live it again." Let us hope that in the presidential elections of 2008 Democrats and Republicans alike will remember the past and finally put Clintonism behind us.

Notes

Prologue

Recruitment by Marshall: Warner, pp. 67-75.
Editorials critical of Nussbaum: *New York Times,* February 27, March 4, 1994.
Efforts to assassinate Castro and others: Church Committee Report, 1975; Hinckle and Turner, pp. 104-223;
Kennedy-Nixon concealment of Cuba project during 1960 presidential campaign: Reeves, chap. 10.
Nixon, Dulles, and U.S. policy in Cuba in 1959-1960: Newman, pp. 113-135.
OSS and CIA recruitment of Mafia members: Hinckle and Turner, p. 289; McCoy, p. 34.

Chapter 1

Zeifman, ch. 1
Washington Post article on Rodino: Drew, p. 114.

Chapter 2

Dean: Zeifman pp. 1-2, 12, 30-32, 34, 38, 49-50, 81, 108, 148, 180, 181, 183, 184, 189

Chapter 3

Discovery of tapes: Woodward and Bernstein pp. 331. 333
Hearings: Senate Select Committee on Campaign Financing Activities, 1973

Chapter 4

Agnew: Zeifman pp. 48-56. 125, 128
Agnew speech to Republican women: Drew, p. 25.
Zeifman, Ch. 6
Fields, pp. 83. 180. 181

Chapter 5

Zeifman, Ch 7

Chapter 6

Doar's decision not to investigate: Breslin, p. 118.
Kennedy amendment to Watergate Committee resolution: Fields, p.34.
Doar's prior positions: Rockefeller Commission Report, pp. 116, 117; Lasky, pp. 199, 212-214, 348, 349, 360, 387-390, 390.

Chapter 7

Zeifman, *Without Honor,* Chs 8-11

Chapter 8

Adler quotes: Adler, p. 78 et seq.
Doar advocacy of "Nurenberg defense:" Judiciary Committee Impeachment Report, p. 382.
Tip O'Neill on delay: O'Neill, p. 252.
Zeifman threatens to resign: Fields, p. 139.

Chapter 9

Zeifman, *Without Honor* Ch 16

Chapter 10

Zeifman, *Without Honor.* Ch 19

Chapter 11

Zeifman, *Without Honor* pp. 212-216

Chapter 12

Janet Reno: Washington Weekly 2/14/00

Chapter 13

Zeifman, *Without Honor* pp. 222-224
Hillarycare: Noonan, *The Case Against Hillary*

Chapter 14

Lasater-Thomasson: Telegraph; World News. May 8. 1994; NewsMax.com 3/16/01; Other crimes: Evans-Pritchard

Chapter 15

Final Report of the Special Committee to Investigate Whitewater Development Corporation and. Related Matters, Senate Report 104 280, 104th Congress, 2d Session

Chapter 16

Jeff Gerth & Stephen Labaton, *Hubbell Receives White House Help*, N.Y. Times 4/10/97

Chapter 17

Creation of Indonesian coal monopoly: Chicago Tribune, *Clinton Critics See Other Motives Behind. Monument Atop Utah Coal,* 12/26/96, P.26; Minneapolis Star Tribune, *This Designation Erupts Plans to Mine World's Largest Deposits of Clean Burning Coal,* 4/30/97 p. 4; Washington Times, Paul.
Craig Roberts, *Utah Coal Deal* 1/12/97. See Also, Ltr. to A.G. Janet Reno from House Judiciary.
Committee Chairman Henry Hyde, 9/3/97.

Chapter 18

Hearings of Senate Committee on Government Affairs; New York Times, John Broder, *Files of Democratic Fund-Raiser,* 4/25/97; Washington Times, Jerry Seper, *Huang Got 109 Classified Briefings,* 4/30/97

Chapter 19

Lifting Trade Embargo on Vietnam::Washintgton Times, Jerry Seper, *Trade With Vietnam,* 12/1/96; U.S. Dept. of State Dispatch 7/10/95
Sibling preference: CNN All Politics, *Lawsuit Fuels Dem Fund-Raising Flap.* 1/16/97

Chapter 20

Schippers, David. *Sell Out.* Regnery, 2000, pp. 38-40, 43-49

Chapter 21

Clinton quotations: CNN All Politics, 2/24/97
New York Times Editorial: July 17, 1997
Woodward Quotation: NBC Meet the Press 7/13/97
Morris quote: Human Events 4/25/97 p27
Soft money transfers to hard money accounts: NY Times, Don Van Natta, *DNC Used Donations for Party in Clinton Re-election Campaign,* 9/10/97
Soft money transfers to states: NY Times, Jill Abramson and . . . Leslie Wayne *Democrats Used the State Parties to Bypass Limits,* 10/2/97
White House Database: House Subcommittee on Gov. Reform, investigative files; Washington Times, Paul Bedard, 5/16/97
Fund-raisers identified: Sen. Com. Gov. evidentiary files; AP 8/27/97
Lincoln Bedroom donors: CNN Allpolitics 2/26/97; NY Times, Don Van Natta. Jr., *Party Officials Orchestrated White House Sleepovers,* 10/4/97
Coffee donors: USA Today, Tom Squitieri, *The Price of Coffee,* 9/16/97
Air Force One and dinner parties: NY Times, Rosenbaum, *White House Fund Raising,* 4/3/97

Chapter 22

Owens, Barbara, *The Final Days,* Regnery 2001

Bibliography

Official Publications (Government Printing Office)

Alleged Assassination Plots Involving Foreign Leaders. Interim Report of the Senate Select. Committee to Study Government Operations with Respect to Intelligence Activities. ("ChurchCommittee"). U.S. Senate, 1975.
Confirmation of Gerald R. Ford as Vice President of the United States. Report of the Committee on the Judiciary, House Report 93-095. 93rd Congress, 1st Session, 1973.
Congressional Directory, 93rd Congress, 2nd Session, 1974.
Impeachment of Richard M. Nixon, President of the United States. Report of the Committee on the Judiciary, U.S. House of Representatives. House Report 93-1305. 93rd Congress, 2nd Session, 1974.
Report to the President by the Commission on CIA Activities, ("Rockefeller Commission") June 1975.
Selected Materials on Impeachment. Committee Print, Committee on the Judiciary, U.S. House of Representatives, 93rd Congress, 1st Session, 1973.
Selected Materials on Impeachment Procedures. Committee Print, Committee on the Judiciary, U.S. House of Representatives, 93rd Congress, 2nd Session, 1974.

Books and Periodicals

Adler, Renata. "Searching for the Real Nixon." Atlantic Monthly, December 1976.
Breslin, Jimmy. *How the Good Guys Finally Won.* New York Viking, 1975.
Clancy, Paul and Shirley Elder. *Tip: A Biography of Thomas O'Neill.* New York: Macmillan, 1980.

Dean, John. *Blind Ambition*. New York: Simon & Schuster, 1976.
Drew, Elizabeth. *Washington Journal* New York: Random House, 1974.
Evans-Pritchard, Ambrose. *The Secret Life of Bill Clinton* 1997
Freemantle, Brian. CIA: *The Honourable Company*. London, Futura, 1983.
Jaworksi, Leon. *The Right and the Power*. New York: Readers Digest, 1976.
Klein, Howard. *The Truth About Hillary*. Sentinel 2005
Lasky, Victor. *It Didn't Start with Watergate*. New York: Dial, 1977.
Noonan, Peggy. *The Case Against Hillary*, Hopper Collins 2000
Olson, Barbara. *Final Day*. Regnery Publishing 2001
O'Neill, Thomas with William Novak. *Man of the House*. New York, Random House, 1987.
Powers, Thomas. *The Man Who Kept the Secrets: Richard Helms and the CIA*, New York: Simon & Schuster, 1979.
Schippers, David. *Sell Out*. Regnery, 2000
Sirica, John. *To Set the Record Straight*. New York: Norton, 1979.
Vann Woodward, C. *Responses of the Presidents to the Charges of Misconduct*. New York: Delacorte, 1974.
Warner, Judith. *Hillary Clinton: The Inside Story*. New York: Penguin, 1993.
Woodward, Robert and Carl Bernstein. *All the President's Me,* New York: Simon & Schuster, 1974.
Zeifman, Jerry. *Without Honor: The Crimes of Camelot and the Impeachment of President Nixon*. Thunders Mouth Press 1995